REDEEMING

VASHTI

Iva J. Frison-Ashe

REDEEMING VASHTI Her Journey From Condemnation to Restoration
Copyright ©May, 2015
by Iva J. Frison-Ashe
Contact us at: Redeemingvashti@gmail.com
Cover & Design: Daan A. Sutherland & Carlos Orta, Jr.
Content Design by: Horace Hord
Library of Congress Cataloging-In-Publication Data
Ashe, Iva J. Frison-Ashe

ISBN-13: 9780991554133
ISBN-10: 0991554132
First Printing May, 2015
Printed in the U.S.A.

This book is dedicated to:

All those who are standing their ground and trusting by Faith in God even when they can't always see through the trials, difficulties, adversities, and challenges of their lives. Our God is Faithful and He will Deliver and Vindicate you! Embrace your journey to Pursue Him, Seek, Serve, and Love Him, with ALL your Heart, Mind, Spirit, Soul, Strength and Might!

The ones who continue to bring so much joy into a life that was struggling for purpose before they arrived and who are the essence of my motivation for why I had to complete my journey today. To Dr. Duane, K. Alexander, Derek, Kylah, Amber, Paris Amber, David Frederick, Ashlee, and Annah.

CONTENTS

ACKNOWLEDGEMENTS & THANKS TO ...

All the Men and Women of God who have ministered and spoken into my life. Whether words of encouragement or ridicule, shame, and condemnation, because it was within the scope of God's Divine Purpose and Plan, I was strengthened and perfected by them all.

My family who always thought that I had too much education to not be a "Doctor, Lawyer, Professor, or some high-titled Business Professional, or government agency official." They were always quick to ask after each course or program of study, "So now what are you qualified to do?" My God! If attitudes and questions like that didn't encourage me to press on. My people, Lord, "I gotta love 'em."

The friends, acquaintances, and colleagues who have entered my life, remained for God's appointed time and season, and then left. LORD Jesus, I thank you.

My children who always encouraged me to fulfill my dream of writing that "story" that was on my heart for over twenty years. They never let me forget that I had to tell it. Even as it evolved from revenge-filled, bitter attacks, to my ultimate surrender, submission, and acquiescence by the power of God's Grace, Peace, and Love. In submitting to a greater story, my hope was that my experiences would strengthen and encourage others, so the choice was made to give God the glory. He certainly showed Himself mighty throughout all that I had witnessed and experienced. Real freedom was realizing that God was indeed in the midst of, and most importantly, orchestrating it all. My children let me know that they had full faith, confidence, and belief in the mother they had grown up with who could do "Anything she set her mind to do."

In addition, not to be considered least. The greatest thanks, gratitude and appreciation goes to the Lord God, His Son Jesus Christ and the power of the Holy Spirit. This dynamic trio ultimately gave me the strength in the formative years of my life to have pressed through all my adversities and challenges. Then, to go on to inspire and encourage that same "press on" spirit in my children, and the many others God placed in my path of influence. Seeing that persevering, the indomitable mindset in their Mom, neighbor, co-worker, mentor, tutor, sister and aunt, allowed them also to see themselves through their adversities, trials, tests, and challenges. They, too, would be able to obtain "all that God had for their lives" -- a Believer's greatest hope, dream, and prayer.

INTRODUCTION

Her life experiences many times gave her the feeling she had extra-sensory encounters. She would have visions and dreams ranging from the sublime to the macabre. She could "see" things. Visions, that when she would first experience them, there would be no reference or anything she could relate them to. However, sure enough, the real-life events would soon happen sending her into that frighteningly strange place that she could never explain to anyone. Into that world that she retreated to for her safety - and sanity. If she held them all in, then no one would know. How was she ever to maneuver through her life's circumstances and situations carrying such a weight? The people she would meet would have no idea or clue to what it was that made her so "strange."

It would be into a life of abuse of trust, lack of integrity, spirits of manipulation and domination for which her birth was destined. Those issues she would have to deal with throughout her lifetime. She would realize that whenever she was posed with either of those offensive circumstances, her portion was that she got more the short end of the interactions. She had been lied to and deceived by close family, friends, and loved ones. So much so until she would become oversensitive to any and all who came to her saying, "Trust me," "I will not betray you"; or "I'll love you forever." There were A few times she decided to "give love a try" and dropped her guard. What happened was only that the betrayal, lie, act of deceit or manipulation repeated – over and over again. Those times gave proof of why she just couldn't, shouldn't and wouldn't ever fully open herself up - to anyone.

Such was the life of the woman who finds herself living a life parallel to that of Queen Vashti. She would never have chosen such a life, but because of choices made by her husband, she too was being called to follow a request that would forever alter her future.

She had a word for others whose choices, walks, and decisions in life have seemed to be in opposition to the prevailing popular mindset and thought patterns. She spoke those words with all peace, grace, humility, and love, "Stand Firm in The Assurance of the Faith To Which You Have Been Called." For who knows, God may be calling you to walk a path that He has designed specifically for you, to fulfill a purpose He will disclose to all at the appointed time.

CHAPTER ONE

CONDEMNATION

*And this is the condemnation, that light is come into the
world, and men loved darkness rather than light,
because their deeds were evil.*
John 3:19

*Therefore as by the offence of one judgment came upon all
men to condemnation; even so by the righteousness of one
the free gift came upon all men unto justification of life.*
Romans 5:18

*All sorrows can be borne if you put them in a story,
or tell a story about them.*
Isak Dinesen

BEGINNING OF SORROWS

To think she would find her life's purpose all intertwined and enmeshed in the story of a disinherited and banished Queen. A Queen dethroned for refusing to comply with the request of her king. A Queen described by many historians as wicked and vain - albeit independent-minded. Though the modern-day Persian meaning of her name translates "sweet-heart," "beloved," "beauty" and "goodness," it was a reconstruction of the Old Persian superlative adjective meaning "excellent woman, best of women" that had this woman so perplexed with the thought that the queen had been presented with such a request.

That request was the exact opposite of Vashti's, but the ultimate outcome would have been the same. She was being asked to disappear from her husband's life, "Just go." It was with great shock and deep disappointment that after more than thirty years, she had not extricated herself from the foolishness that was her marriage. That day of her wedding had been the worst ceremonial acknowledgment of matrimony she had ever witnessed; say nothing of being a participant - albeit ambivalent and doubt filled.

She and Marshall had gotten married in 1977. She was twenty-two years old, and he was thirty-six. She had been considered mature beyond her years, but the reality and truth of her immaturity were quickly realized as she undertook the role of being Marshall's wife. The weight and magnitude of what she had embarked upon caused her great doubt. Still, for all the reasons she had endured the years of her marriage, she could not comprehend such a request as was presented to The Queen, nor would or could she ever consider complying.

1

Besides, she did not see herself as wicked in any way – focused, finally structured and determined after years of growing up in chaos, and indiscipline, yes – but never wicked. Nevertheless, it brought judgment and condemnation upon her. (John 3:19) That she would just walk away from what she had sacrificed, all those years of her youth was incomprehensible and unconscionable.

Vashti's life-altering experience was taking place after raising four children, setting up and managing four different homes, and enduring triumphantly over life-threatening attacks to both her health and sanity. That she would find herself becoming a widow in her mid-life at the age of fifty-two was something she had never, imagined. Sure, Marshall's dying during the time when it was being planned that she would be "removed" and "replaced," should have cut short or even ended, her experience – or so she thought. Her offense had brought such great judgment upon her that even after his death, the attacks persisted – actually intensifying all the more. There would be consequences and repercussions she would have to endure. Her actions, or lack thereof, were being seen as blatant disobedience and rebellion. Her justification could come through only one but she was so far from him now. (Rom 5:18)

SELF-MADE LIFE MAPS AND PLANS

There was a map she had laid out for her life, a Plan "A" that would assure happiness, and success, wealth and prosperity. However, after encountering the hindrances and obstacles her husband had placed upon her to prevent and deny her from accomplishing any of them, she was now on Alternate Plan Double Z-B99. She had lost all hope of ever attaining to that place of true happiness and fulfillment she so longed for and desired. Following Marshall's death, she would eventually experience a short period of wealth and prosperity, but would allow her sense of needing to rescue the world to cause her to lose it all.

She could vividly recall the many situations and circumstances that had happened to her starting way back to the very beginning of their relationship that got her to the Plan Double Z-B99 place and time she was now. She had poured herself into the façade of their marriage fearing getting married presented the only respectable and viable alternative for her at the time. In addition, when those times became one painful year after another, she was too embroiled in the day-today of it all to give serious contemplation to extricating herself. Where they were now when all was beginning to unravel, was at the place of Marshall's forced retirement from his employer of thirty years - and their resulting money challenges.

She had seen it all along, a drastic change in his employment happening. He was the major breadwinner for their family, and that was because he was so insecure with her being out in public without him. He witnessed her become that

3

self-assured and confident woman she was when they had first met. That was the woman she transformed into – the one she was always meant to be - whenever she did venture outside of her home. That woman was too much of a threat to Marshall.

Therefore, she had resolved to be the mother and homemaker that kept the conflicts to a minimum. For there was no appeasing a man determined to keep you from fulfilling who you were meant to be. Actually, everything would threaten his security - whether she was employed outside of their home or managing the affairs of their lives and children inside that home.

Her children. They were the true joy of her life and looking after them is what enabled her to endure all those years. There was an innate "mother's nature" in her and nurturing and giving her all to them is what nourished it. She gave her life for the fulfilling of their lives. They did not ask to be born into such dysfunction. She owed it to all four to help get them to the places of success, and accomplishment God had destined for their lives.

So, when her pleas to Marshall that they down-size their life-style fell on his deaf ears, she was not surprised. She was determined to brace herself and prepare for the hardships that she had been shown were sure to come. That she couldn't explain to him, her husband of all those years how she had been warned in dreams and visions that their lives were about to be upset and drastically changed, hurt her deeply.

She needed help with the weight of what she was carrying, but realized early on that Marshall would not be that one to help her. His spiritual maturity was taking a little longer than she had patience for, but her promise to God to love his son into the man of God he desired him become allowed her to endure more than she thought possible.

She had learned through the years that her love language was communicating. If she could talk and express her concerns, it made her a much happier woman. The man she was married to for all these years had no understanding of the gift God had placed inside of her. It didn't matter that she had shared with him so many of those visions and dreams - and they all came true.

Those visions and dreams were continuing to give warning of situations which would have severe impact and consequences regarding their first two children going off to college; the last two encountering a myriad of life challenges; and then, her three-year physical, mental and emotional illness. Because God had pre-warned her, she was able to buffer her children and remain peaceful and focused during all their adversities.

The eldest of their sons had made it through his last year of high school and managed to remain focused. He had become too attached to a girlfriend and their relationship was threatening his desire to go off to college. It didn't help that Marshall supported their son's misguided and short-sighted decision, this mother took the matter into her own hands, made sure all his paperwork was submitted, packed up his bags and drove him herself. He would spend the next six years obtaining his bachelor of science and then his doctorate of medical degrees.

When it looked like partying would interfere with his completing his final year of school is when the lord showed her to warn that son that he should never leave a drink unattended. It was a three a.m. phone call to that young man who was just coming in from a night of wild college fun.

"I need you to listen to me carefully, son, this is critically important."

"Yeah, Mom. I hear you."

"Whenever you go out. Never, ever leave anything you're eating or drinking. Always stay with it until you finish it. Do you understand what I'm saying? I need you to promise me."

"Ma, is everything alright?"

That was my children's' way of saying to me, "You're weirding out on me right now, Ma. There's more you want to me know, so spill it."

"Well, I had a dream that you had drank something while you were out and it made you so sick that you had to go to the hospital. I made myself wake up from that dream because I was sweating and my heart was pounding out of my chest from fear. With how awful I was feeling during that dream, I didn't want to experience the outcome of your hospital stay. So, I called you right away."

"Tell me. Promise me you'll never leave anything you're eating or drinking unattended. Don't try covering it up or even asking a buddy or friend to watch it for you. Please be careful, son."

"Mom, I got it. I understand. Don't worry."

So, when his younger brother who, for reasons to be explained later, reluctantly left for that same college, called to say, "Mom, don't get upset. But my brother is in the emergency room. I was called by one of his friends to a club they were at. Mom, he's my big brother and I can't take seeing him like this. It's so scary, Mom, I wish you were here. They said he was stumbling around, mumbling and slurring his speech, sweating and throwing up. He had ordered a drink and before finishing it, got in a dance to his favorite jam. They said when he got back to their table and finished that drink, he still seemed to be having a real good time. But then, after a few minutes, he started throwing up and mumbling stuff."

Oh, my dear God! Which do I address first? I got a younger child scared to death and trying to look after his older brother. And I've got that older brother possibly fighting for his life three hundred miles away from me.

When I first had that dream about leaving drinks or food unattended, after calling my oldest son, the second person I called was my second-born. He was a natural-born nurturer and caregiver who had the greatest calm and composure when facing challenges. I had confided the dream to him and asked that he look out for his older brother. He wasn't the partying type though, and would not have accompanied his big bro to the place where he was that night. When he told me, "Mom, my brother kept saying, I didn't leave it but for a minute. I didn't mean to leave it. She told me not to."

My younger son reported to me that - as it felt like my breathing had totally stopped or that I was holding my breath throughout his entire recanting of events - the hospital had just let him know that his brother would be fine, thanks to getting him there so quickly. There it was back again, I felt my breathing return.

Then, at another time, after another dream, this same second son received a call from me in the wee hours of the morning. Again the message had the same urgency and overwhelming sense of impending danger and possible harm - only this time there was the feeling of a greater threat.

"I know you know that what I'm about to say, you have to follow exactly. Do not allow anyone into your car, Son. If they need to get somewhere, give them the keys and let them have it." Those words sounded strange to say even to me, but I was following as I had been directed in this new dream. This son had just recently purchased his very own first car and was known for helping out his roommates, friends or whoever needed a ride. So, I could only pray that he heeded the warning.

What transpired to affirm the validity of what God had shown me was when a childhood friend of his asked for a ride back home in the early wee hours one morning. He would tell me later that, "Mom, first I remembered what you had told me. Then, because it was so early in the morning, I knew something had to be up that wasn't good. And finally, I had exams that morning and didn't want to miss them. Anyway, I gave him money to take a cab to the bus terminal and told him that was the best I could do. It was hard, Mom, but I'm glad I did, cause later that morning we heard on the news that a tragic accident had happened on campus that night and it was in the same dorm that my friend lived in. Police were involved and questioning everybody."

Then again, shortly after that incident, he was pulled up at a convenience store and two guys approached him. One of them barked at him to get out of his car. The six-foot-four All-American male in my son answered, "Man, what's up with you?" That's when the other guy pulled out a shotgun and said,

"You heard me. I aught to shoot you right now. Give me dem car keys."

At that point is when my very brave son remembered, "Nothing is worth your life" and after telling the guys, "Sure, just let me step out and it's yours."

He would tell me that once he collected himself and could call me, those guys had both been killed by police after robbing and shooting two other people.

Yes, there were countless other dreams - not always of doom and gloom but of great blessings and accomplishments. These two situations are only a couple, but there were many things God was showing me that actually came forth.

It was Marshall's directive for me to take the lead in interacting with everybody and every situation. I always did, too - although reluctantly. Now that he was gone, I looked forward to never having to make another major decision on my own all by myself.

Vashti vowed to hold fast to filling the rest of her life with those pleasures and experiences she had missed in her years with Marshall. Those that brought her as much joy and thrills as possible. That was, of course before she received her life-altering, destiny-defining and life-changing assignment.

A "GOD" ASSIGNMENT

It had taken less than maybe six months after Marshall's passing for her to feel the strength of her body and mind return. Then, to think about fixing herself up and dressing in something more than sweat pants and a top or one of her granny house dresses. She had been the one to choose to live a health-conscious lifestyle for the past few years, and especially since Marshall's diagnosis. He had always insisted on the both of them eating heavy, always including some white flour-based, breaded, deep-fried and carb-heavy food.

However, when she was strong enough and smart enough to refuse to eat the same as he did, she began to see a marked improvement in her health. And, as a result, she was enjoying the benefits of the new trend in how aging was viewed. Thirty, being the new twenty; forty, the new thirty; and her fifty-two, the new forty-two.

There was an exception in her case, however. Maybe it was because she had gotten back into making up her face and playing around with different hairstyles and all that was accentuating her best features. So, many were saying she looked more to be in her mid-to-late- thirties instead. Were it not for her feeling the aches and pains from each one of those fifty-two years, most days, she would agree and answer to maybe thirty-six or thirty-eight.

Sadly, she could not begin to assign the same qualities to her level of emotional maturity. That deficit in her maturity had kept pace with neither her mid-life age of fifty-two nor the complimentary assignment of forty-two. It was especially difficult when she considered all she had endured in her formative years. Therefore, to add in the last thirty of being married to Marshall, she felt certain instead she had surely lost several years' of potential growth. As she thought it over, when she considered her maturity in matters of her relational intimacy, it was no surprise that she felt no more developed than a high school freshman. That was sad indeed. But, there was so much she had not experienced where she would have been able to employ learned life and interpersonal skills.

She knew there was a woman inside of her who was desperate to know how to respond to the trials of life she was about to encounter. A veiled woman was secretly hidden away, waiting to be released. But, the woman who had come to where she had, and through what she had, had never become proficient in the life skills she would now need. That woman had repeatedly and constantly been denied that opportunity during her fifty-two years to develop. How it happened that her progress was thwarted was a battle she felt she had surely lost at the cost of maintaining her sanity and life itself. There seemed to be some unseen force working against her in both those areas of her life – even before her birth.

BIRTH OF THE TWINS

Frequent memories beginning even before her birth were very troublesome. She was right, however, a great battle had started before she would be born. There was indeed a plan afloat to take her out, and it was put in place before she was even ever conceived. It would be her chance meeting one day with a nurse at the county hospital who would recognize her name as she confirmed the spelling of it with the desk assistant, she heard, "Iz dat whut ya' say ya name iz?"

Before she could answer, the woman had spoken my maiden name and given the loudest yell she could – taking into consideration that she was in a place of business – a medical facility at that. "Yes," I responded. "That is my name. "Do I know you?" "Ya shouldn't know me at all. But I rememba ya and yar sista. Ya're a twin."

Most people in the city knew that. Therefore, this woman wasn't shedding much light on how it was she knew me, until, she went into a full recap of the day my sister, and I were born. As I listened intently, I had to translate quickly as this woman, in all her enthusiasm and excitement, was going back and forth from perfect English, one sentence to islander's speech the next. She was speaking excessively fast for my non-Island-reared ears. There was a thrilled amazement and wonder in her voice that caused her words to slur together as she began her account of that day.

"The day was Friday the 26th of November in the winter of 1954 and, the day after Thanksgiving Day – how ironic. We nurses had no idea twins were arriving. I was the most recent nurse on the staff just having just arrived from Jamaica and was assigned to that twenty year old mother-soon-to-be, your Mama. There was something I saw in that young woman that caused me to quickly give up on the idea of having another take it easy night we all had hoped for. Had I been totally honest with myself, I would have heeded the spirit's warning and known definitely not to anticipate such a night."

"I had been having visions of myself in that exact situation with a young lady about to give birth for some time, even months, before your mother walked in. It may have been no more than five minutes before, but in my dreams, I had experienced the precise circumstances of her arrival that night. What I can truthfully tell you now is that what I saw was a pregnant woman entering the emergency room," and, she continued as she looked at me knowingly, "because you seem like you can understand and know what it is I am talking about, there was a 'presence' with her. No one else but me saw it though."

"And don't you know, just as that whole scene ended, your mother arrived -- and with her that 'thing' that walked alongside her. It shocked me so that I turned to my co-worker to ask, "Do you see that thing that just came in the door?"

She responded jokingly, "Now Claudette, you don't want to get written up. You remember they told us we were not supposed to refer to the patients in terms like that." Because I had witnessed other similar presences and tried to share with my co-workers, I knew well what she was talking about. However, I realized this nurse had no clue as to what it was I

13

had just witnessed. Like if I had seen in my dream, only I would see that 'thing.'

Nurse Claudette continued, "I know. You're right," I told my co-worker so as not try explaining the whole situation. "Still though, I looked outside and down the hallways to double check that my eyes had not tricked me. I was sure they had not because there had been times before in my homeland that the same thing had happened – many times before. My parents had wanted for me to carry on and devote myself to the dark arts they were into. I just could not." My turnaround had come when my little town was visited by a missionary team of young adults who told us about a Savior who was Jesus who came to the earth so that we could be free from everything. I took them literally at their word and applied it to every area of my life; especially the practices my parents were involved in.

So, it appeared that I was the only one to see that dark-spirited entity and no one else could be found who had come in with your mother, or who had dropped her off. That had been the first thing for my co-workers that was too unusual about this birth we would be attending to. But the second for me, of course thanks to that spirit walking through the door, that was too unusual was that there was no husband, no mother, no sisters or brothers, nobody. She was twice the size of a normal woman ready for delivery and should have had some type help. Then, as she was being examined, there were the unusual scarring and gouges, nicks and cuts around her birthing area. When we asked her, 'How in the world did those scars happen?' She gave no explanation. "But don't you know,

14

I persisted. It didn't matter none to me, 'cause this nurse knew the signs and this young mother was demonstrating them all."

"She had tried to terminate this pregnancy and I knew why," Nurse Claudette continued. "That poor young mother could sense that there was a spiritual battle taking place within her womb and it terrified her. I could only guess at what she had done, or at what had been done to her. What door had been opened to cause such a thing?"

"Back home they would say that it was because your mother and/or your father had disobeyed and rebelled against the spirits and had a mojo placed on them. But me, this nurse knew different. Someone had made a pact with the enemy. An agreement made with the devil to give you two precious babies in exchange for the gifts that were inside of you both. What earthly possession could have possibly been so valuable and worth more to own. What hurt, harm or pain could, either your father or mother, whichever one of them it was, have experienced, suffered or endured that had opened the door allowing and causing them to sell off their very souls in exchange for you two precious ones. Or, just maybe, the enemy knew there was a special something to come forth from you babies and he was purposing to kill it before it could take its first breath."

"Your young mother must have known for months that there were two to be born from her and that made it even harder for her as she tried to get rid of you. She had confided in me alone later that night when I questioned her, all the things she had tried. None of them had worked, thank God - not jumping and falling down real hard, not drinking bottles of castor oil and vinegar, and not even her attempts to pierce the bag that held the two of you ever so securely in her body. Nothing worked. She only succeeded in causing herself severe pain and profuse bleeding. So that when she'd gone back home to her Mama's, your grandmother, and her mother had no idea or clue of the number times, your Mama had tried to undo the situation she was in. I guess no one ever found out that your mother had tried to do away with the two of you, eh?" I interjected, "Not until years later Nurse Claudette.

When she was so frustrated and irritated with us girls, she said, "'I should have done away with your asses when I had a chance.'" "And since she got frustrated easily and often, it always hurt so badly when Mama would say things like that."

With a look of sincere sympathy in her eyes, Nurse Claudette continued, "My experience observing these kinds of things in my country helped me to recognize that there was a spirit of raw, resident evil over your mother; and she wasn't fighting against it either. It was as she was in complete agreement. I wondered what could have possibly happened to open her up to receive this deadly spirit – because it was known to come only to kill, steal and destroy (John 10:10). It sometimes caused young weak ones to take not only the lives of the unborn, but their own lives as well -- usually a real bloody mess. Thus stealing the life potential for God's glory to be manifested, and destroying God's plan. Your mother had not succeeded with dislodging you two babies, though. You guys were somehow holding on for dear life."

She went on, "I can remember it like it was just yesterday. As I ran the stethoscope over her belly, I asked her,

'Mommy, ya know ya got yourself two healthy thriving babies here, dear? No one ever tell ya dat? Ya been having a hard time of it dear? How is it ya got so many marks down dere?' She had slipped in and out of her Island dialect so I had to listen more intently as she continued her story. "Course I knew all too well what those marks meant. Something was making it more worth your Mom's while to bring two innocent lives to a premature grave rather than to their healthy births and lives of hope and a future. (Jeremiah 29:11) Who could it be? What could it be?

Why was it so determined to put an end to your lives?"

"In all that pain she was in, your Mom still took the strength to tell me," 'Leave me alone lady and just get these damned things out of me.' "Only this time, now she was screaming it." "It's gonna take a while longer dear. Ya gonna be alright but you gonna have to help us keep these babies safe for right now. Ya do dat and Nurse Claudette promises she'll take real good care of ya all." 'Lady I ain't promising you nothing. If I'd had my way, I wouldn't even be here right now.' "I know dear and dat's real, real sad," Nurse Claudette said she told my mother.

"Our Nurse's station desk clock chimed twelve midnight as the first of you twins silently emerged. I can tell even now it was your sister and not you who was first born. That helped me to come up with your names, too. I didn't even know if your mama had names chosen for you or not. But for your sister, I chose a delicate and dainty flower. She was fragile and only offered a faint whimper when she was smacked on her bottom by the doctor. Now you were a totally different

17

story. So, while we were cleaning up your big sister, it was exactly five minutes later that you forcefully popped into the world with eyes ablaze, flailing about and screaming full throttle like the weight of the world had been thrust upon your little shoulders."

"You were clearly much smaller than your sister, but your size was not a factor in the level and volume of your demonstrating the full functioning of your lungs for us all. You let heaven and earth know that you had made it on the scene in all your glory. There was another big thing that was different about you, baby, and those interns assisting in delivering you two would not have a clue what it meant. Sure, they could recite the medical terms for it, but there was a deeper and more important spiritual meaning than anything from our PDR Book. It was what confirmed so many things that had been put in place and into play. One being, why it was I chose the profession I did and had been drawn to this country, landing a position in this specific hospital. It confirmed also, why your mother appeared at this hospital on this very night. You see, I was scheduled to be off the next day for my two-week vacation. I had to cancel those plans now.

Another thing that was the confirmation of all my suspicions about why that thing had walked through the hospital doors with your mother. It was the corroboration of why your mother was so troubled and why it was that something had tried to have her to get rid of you both before; you were able to take your first breaths. And most importantly, it had confirmed why, too, I had been led to immediately pray and place a covering over the two of you babies as quickly as I could, and for as many times after as I could get to you.

The 'it' was the 'Veil' that was over your little face. It had great meaning and carried much weight in my country. I had seen it so many times and wouldn't discount its power in this country either. There would be two forces working in your precious life to wreak havoc and devastation in everything you did. There would be spirits you would not even be aware of like rejection, abandonment, self-sabotage, depression, inferiority, oversensitivity to the opinions of others, and maintaining focus and clarity about your life's purpose. With a mother like yours, I did not give you much of a chance at overcoming, or triumphing and getting the victory over any of them; but I still prayed that you would.

You, my child, would need a special invoking of prayer for protection. The same prayers that helped me to get away from the forces I grew up around and that had many times threatened to destroy me and take me out. My child, yes, this nurse's battle had been great, but it would be like a schoolyard game compared to what lay ahead for you two little ones; and especially you. So, I would go to the Father over and over again praying, "

"Father God, protect these little ones in the situations they will find themselves. Let no hurt or harm utterly destroy what you have placed in them; especially the one you've marked. Keep her shielded and strengthen her for the assignment you've placed within her. Let her neither abort nor miscarry. Fill them both with your Word and let your Holy Spirit ever reside in them. Let them both grow in patience and strengthen their endurance so that in their due seasons, they will bring forth all that you've placed in them. Amen"

"That would be my prayer for the five days your Mom was at the hospital. I could not help but come in early every one of those days to spend as much time with the two of you as I could. I recognized I, too, was on an assignment and that your future well-being was upon my not failing. It was after I first prayed that prayer that I asked your mother what names she had for her baby girls."

"I ain't got no names," was her response. I knew I was taking great liberties, but I told her, "I have two perfect names for your girls? I wanted to say to your motha', "Your two beautiful baby girls. But my dear, no offense, ya' both looked like little rats. Just like lil' mice. Did you ever see a picture of ya'selves when ya' was just born? Ya' Mom didn't agree to let us nurses take any with the Polaroid cameras we had. But the Doctor who delivered ya'll, Dr. Shirley, he insisted on getting your pictures. You all were the very first twins to be born at our little hospital, you know. So he had us to get some shots of you whenever your Mom wasn't aware. That Dr. Shirley would recall for years to come, how there was a set of twins living right here in our city who had been the very first he would deliver at this hospital. He would be pleased to know you were faring well."

"So," let me continue, "Your Mom never knew about those pictures, but I thought I'd sneak one of them into her papers hospital discharge papers just in case, maybe she had a change of heart later.

Ah, ha! That's what the inquisitive me found as I was rummaging through my Mom's things years ago; a picture of two of the saddest-looking newborns ever. Nurse Claudette was so right. We had the kind of baby faces you would gaze at and search for the right words to express what it was you were beholding. Finally, you'd realize that all you could muster was a, "Oooooh! What... a... precious... baby!" And leave it at that. I can recall hearing that a lot from different people as a little one. But they all turned to, "Oh, they are so cute," about the age of three or four. Thank God!

I didn't include all of that in my response to her question about the picture, so she continued, "Anyway, your mother told me about your names,"

"Don't make no difference to me, whatever you say will do just fine.' "I had succeeded in conveying by declaration and decree of your names, the life assignments God had shown me you two would have. One of you would be like a delicate and water-sensitive (cleansing and purifying, life giving) flower. It would be a tearfulness that would distinguish her. Although outwardly, your sister appeared fragile and vulnerable, she was strong-spirited inside. So, for her to cry at the drop of a hat was really something. Your twin would be marked by her sensitivity to the hearts of my people and would respond in either smiles of joy and gladness, or the saddest tearfulness.

God had shown me that if, in the time he sent her to his people she found them fulfilling his plan for the work his son did, she would blossom and flourish. But, if she found them lacking in any way, the waters of her heart and soul would flow forth in unending torrents. Her tears would be never-ending."

"And then, for you, the veiled one. Your name was to be as God had given in my time of prayer, meditation, and researching the Word. What I had found was that although sometimes associated in the stories of Greek mythological characters, your name appeared as that of the Greek goddess who transported messages between mortals and the Mount Olympus Deities. God let me know that indeed your assignment would entail your bearing a message, but the name's main interpretation that God had to stick in my spirit was the biblical Hebrew meaning of "God is gracious," "Gift of God," "God's Grace" and "one who exposed, revealed, uncovered, disclosed light and brought sunlight."

"You, little one would bear the burden of delivering a message of all messages - and only by and through the grace and mercy of God Almighty. Your personality and character would be so deeply and intricately woven into your life's earthly day-to-day duties, and spiritual, end-times purpose and mission, that you would most likely confuse them both. You may even have to bear the reproach of one having a psychological maladjustment. Every aspect of your life would be impacted by this character trait. Many people would find it offensive and intrusive. How dare you bring up their hidden faults and failings? Even if your disclosure to them was done ever so innocently and in a manner hoping to help them. The chances of your completing this assignment would depend greatly upon you staying true to yourself and keeping your heart free. Any entanglements that did not enhance and promote your assignment would forestall, hinder, cause you to abort and miscarry; and possibly even worse, bring on your untimely death."

"What a faithful God we have that he has not allowed the enemy to your destiny and assignment to take your life. There must be something so special about you my child that He would entrust this to you. You are still here and please tell me that you know what I'm talking about. You too understand the magnitude of what has been placed on your life. Our meeting here today cannot be by accident, but a Divine appointment. I am here for you to strategically help you make it through. Now tell Nurse Claudette, "How are you fairing?"

"How could I confide in this woman the truth of where it was I actually found myself? Lost, confused and unsure of anything. Now, thanks to her reciting of events, I unknowingly also bore generational curses from whatever my mother and father had done. Added to all that was the fact that I was certifiably "different" and "strange." She was right about that psychological thing too. I had been diagnosed with everything from a Borderline Personality Disorder with a Sad Affect; or, like most psychiatrists like to diagnose, Manic Depressive Disorder and Paranoid Schizophrenic. Psychology Today in its online Diagnosis Dictionary describes Bipolar Disorder as:

> *A Manic-Depressive illness characterized by severe mood shifts or a mix of depression, anxiety, and high-energy delusional phases known as manic episodes. It is a brain disorder that causes unusual shifts in mood, energy, and ability to function. These are not*

the normal ups and downs; the symptoms of bipolar disorder are severe. They can result in damaged relationships, poor job or school performance, and even suicide. www.themoorings.org/life/family /marriage/knowledge.html

That information explained so much for me concerning my interactions in most all my relationships, employment history and school performance. I had proven to be an intelligent and above-average student; but, if ever overwhelmed, it took the greatest of struggles for me to get back on track. One thing I had successfully fought off was all thoughts of self-hurt or suicide. It must have been that I recognized there was some battle within myself and I was by no means or circumstances, about to let whatever force it was that said, "Just kill yourself," win over my greatest desire to live and thrive.

So, the fact that I, this second-born twin, was now aware of my condition, did not bring comfort, per se. What it did was to offer explanations as to why, no matter what I tried to do to keep myself from going into a slump of emotions, I would sometimes still be overcome by tearfulness or brief bouts of sadness. It was the greatest of my emotional and psychological battles. At this stage of my life though, I had control of the most severe of my mood swings. What I had been able to do in accomplishing some semblance of control was to minimize those occurrences so that, yes, they did occur, despite my many attempts to thwart them. But, their occurrences did not take total control of me as at first. My symptoms seemed worse than ever when I was under emotional stress. Stressors from work, or performance of any other type I seemed to manage well. It was when my heart was involved that all control was lost and those emotions wreaked havoc with my ability to maintain all semblance of psychological balance.

Therefore, this was another reason it seemed all the more plausible for me, this twin born veiled, to be shielded in a loving marriage where my husband would have been my covering and protect me from the hazards of the world. The way it worked in the novels, movies and television programs... right.

I continued my attempt to explain to Nurse Claudette. "Then, there were the similarities to my marriage and the dethroned Queen Vashti that fueled the gnawing, deep-rooted feelings inside of me that there was something I had to accomplish that was so much bigger than my little personal self-fulfillment issues."

How was she fairing -- indeed. Nurse Claudette's question and her showing up couldn't have happened at a more apropos, opportune and critically needed time. The nurse would now walk with me as my mother figure, Mentor, personal confidante and the Godly counsel I desperately needed - and had to have if I was to continue to make it through successfully. Nurse Claudette would become this one's lifeline.

HER PARENTS

My mother and father would both be strikingly attractive, with impressive and statuesque physiques. They could have easily been considered the Shamar Moore and Beyoncé of their day. Both were witty and smart – he, book smart, and she, street smart.

Though I was the second-born twin, that fact did not deter me from assuming the role of elder twin. It wasn't a subtle displacement of my sister either. It seemed everything I did had a take-charge flare and fiery excitement to it. That was my true and honest, unadulterated nature. The blazing light of my personality would illuminate wherever I was and whatever it was, I was doing. What I learned was that it could very well have been an inherited trait from my dad's father. My grandfather - a man with a hell-fueled, fiery, explosive, and uncontrollable temper. This grandfather exhibited a generally all-around depraved disposition.

From all I had learned of that grandfather, and what I did not care to emulate, was that he was not faithful in anything he engaged in, lacked establishing goals or having ambitions of any kind. He would epitomize the statement that "the only things to come out of Key West were conchs, punks, and drunks." His major weakness, besides his horrible personality, would be drinking. He became known as a messy, fist-fight loving, hell-raising drunk who indulged way beyond any levels of acceptable excess.

When I learned about him, my vow was to not allow myself to follow any of his faults and failings. I would have a plan for my life. I would not allow myself to become so addicted to anything that it would cause me to lose sense of who I was. In addition, most importantly, I would not ever allow myself to cover up or repress that part of me that was my essence, my spiritual gifting – what it was that caused things to become revealed and uncovered.

Even though it was when I would let that element of myself loose that I encountered the greatest confrontational adversities; especially from those whose actions my walking in the reality of what I was, exposed who they were. Although I found my greatest self-fulfillment at those times when that giftedness of mine was in operation, the weight of it all was just too much for me to bear. I would not know until years later how to handle those extremely uncomfortable situations.

It was my paternal grandmother who was a hardworking and quiet country girl of African-American, Native American and French descent – wholesome and beautiful. She would wrongly assume that the young man she had met in their west-coast naval base city was hard working, conscientious, and respectful. After all, he was in the navy and had to be a cut above the rest, is what she had heard and had thought. She didn't allow herself the time to observe any of his other characteristics – the ones he had just beneath the surface, in hiding. His looks and outgoing personality were so very overpowering. Had she given herself the time to do so, she could have at least discerned some degree of the hell-fired man that he was.

Fortunately, it would not take her too long after meeting him to discover his secret vice -- his alcoholism – albeit not soon enough. It was on their second date when he had switched out from sober and self-controlled, to one who after three drinks, had turned into a raging sexual deviate. He violated her and the result nine months later was the birth of my father -- a child he never really wanted anything to do with. It was always and only so that his destructive and deadly spirits could and would be forever in control of the woman's God-fearing spirit. It was my grandmother's life and soul he was after.

My grandmother's parents were faithful believers in God and had insisted that she marry that young man. It would be the worst advice of her parents she would ever obediently follow. Immediately, the beatings and abuse began. That young woman would spare no details in letting her growing son know just how it was he was conceived. It would allow her father to swear he would never follow the ways of that Key-Wester. He would be different. He would be better.

It was at the point of his young adult life when my father had met my mother and had developed a great relationship and love for God and His Word. He could recite whole passages of scripture. He had met my mother when on a path set for him by God himself. He knew it. His mother knew it. Everyone knew he was chosen by God to be a minister of His Word. My father did realize too, from the history of his beginning, that he had to tread a much different path from that of his father or else he was on track to repeat the very same and exact life issue errors that caused him to be born.

He realized that inside of him was a spirit with the potential for irreverence, and of being explosive and uncontrollable. If he ever allowed himself to be filled with enough alcohol to cause him to forget his life assignment, then he, too, had the potential to revert to those very same actions of his father. He too would become an uncontrolled and depraved despot. He too, would revere nothing. He would respect nothing and no one.

So, since my father had sworn never to take a drink of alcohol, he felt himself safe from the one vice that could snare him into defaulting from his life's path. He was determined not to allow himself to give in to his father's faults and failings. He knew oh too well the story of just what resulted in his mother dropping her guard and having come under the influence of a heavy spirit of drunkenness to forcibly overcome her.

So, my dad chose a different path. His mother had done all she could to insure that he would. Besides, when he had heard the words of forgiveness and deliverance by the grace and mercy of God through the saving and sanctifying power and blood of Jesus Christ by his sacrifice on the cross, he knew he wanted - no, he needed and had to have that.

The female contributor to my birth and one into whose womb I was supposed to be nourished and protected had a long sad story of abandonment, abuse, rejection, social dysfunction, anger, and bitterness. She, herself a twin, found herself still living in the home of her parents. It would be my mother's mother then, who was caught up in trying to not only work alongside her farm day-laborer husband, while managing her home; but who also undertook the care for me, my twin and two older sisters. Added to that overload were three children of my mother's twin who were dropped off at our grandmother's house every day.

So, by the time my twin and I came along, our mother had decided to take off to destinies unknown to us. Yes, that left us abandoned as young as newborns with no time or opportunity for our grandmother to give to us the love and care we needed, and deserved. Although, because we were twins, like our grandmother was too, we received as much favoritism from her as was possible. I would learn it was a vicious cycle repeating itself throughout our generations – for neither had our mother been cared for or protected by that same woman, our grandmother.

It was at the place our mother now found herself after returning to collect us that she was attempting to make more of her life by attending beauty school. She heard that there was love, acceptance, and forgiveness in coming to a loving God. She so wanted that love after having allowed herself too many times before to be in bad places responding negatively to her anger and hurt. Those instances had twice resulted in her bringing forth babies.

Our mother was so young and was not even able to identify or verbalize, or say nothing to attempt to resolve her life issues for herself. We babies, the twins, and our two older sisters (older by two and three years), would go through many of the same trials and hardships our mother had experienced. There were men in our mother's family who had no respect for the innocence and frailty of young ones and took advantage of us innocent ones every opportunity they could.

At the time, my mother had met my father, she had resolved through suppression, repressed and hidden anger, much of her pain, resentment, and rage. Therefore, on the surface, at least, many of her issues were not easily discerned or obvious. It took just a closer look to uncover the spirits of deep-rooted hostility and bitterness lying beneath the facade of her gorgeously taut skin. That she could hide her true countenance and instead appear open, friendly, and inviting was a mystery. She even presented herself as willing to allow the Word of God to do a work in her life - and the changes were showing. Until...

Until she met him, my father. Both my mother and father would forsake their walks in and by the Spirit of God and relinquish control instead to the carnal spirits battling valiantly for ownership of their bodies. My father would forsake his path of minister-in-training; and she would forsake her walk as a freshly converted Believer. They allowed their passions to arise and overpower them, for fulfillment of their flesh. Although they both knew better, they were helpless to fight against, or to resist, those raging desires.

It was at a revival they both attended where he would ask her out on a date to the movies. The only movie theater they could attend at the time was on Seventh Avenue and Fourth Street. He had no way of knowing she had never ever attended a theater before. Although she had definitely heard the stories of what went on in the balcony seats, though. However, she felt no reason to believe that what happened for the other young women would ever happen to her. She would be with a handsome young minister in training and had no need to worry about anything like that befalling her. This was her chance to escape her fast downward-spiraling life. It was going full speed and this relationship would be her big opportunity to escape the inevitable life that awaited someone like her. She had great hopes for this first date.

Unfortunately, she had no way of knowing that there was no "happily ever after" in the future for them. Theirs would be a clash of the classes. He was the only son in a family who had put great emphasis on his succeeding in his education, who owned considerable property, a home, and cars and were well established in their local church body and community.

She was the daughter of day laborers who followed the harvesting of crops leaving in the earliest hours of the morning to get to the fields and sometimes the groves as far away as Central and West Florida. Her mother's parents rented the three-bedroom shanty from the same farmers they worked for. During the daytime, the three children of my mother's twin sister were at the house as well. It was amazing that by the time, my twin and I came along and began to get around on our own and walking about, that small house didn't feel cramped at all. It would be the only place we would know as "home" for the first nearly four years of our lives.

Education was a catch as catch can situation in my grandmother and grandfather's household. Depending on how the crops were, sometimes it took as many in the house who were big enough, to help harvest whatever fruit or vegetable crop in their tri-county cities needed harvesting. Her grandmother and grandfather had to make sure the family had enough money to meet their needs. By the time, my mother would graduate high school she, having not been the best of students was ready to give birth to the first of her five daughters. She would roll in beauty school following the second daughter's birth that next year. It was the energy and liveliness of the women she found herself around that inspired her to desire a better life. It had been the women of that beauty training school who had invited her to the Revival where she met Marshall.

Everyone on her street was looking out his or her doors or windows as that handsome young man pulled up in his immaculately shining and clean auto to collect his date. It wouldn't be until much later that he would find out she was the mother of two toddlers. That fact wouldn't matter to him at all though, because he never considered this young woman could ever be something acceptable to his discriminating parents. Though he was sure that she, as beautiful and attractive in every inch of her statuesque and voluptuous body was as infatuated and taken with him as he was with her. He was right. Their union would cause him to deny his place, his calling, and assignment and produce not one, but two innocent seeds. I would be one of those soon to be besieged and beleaguered seeds.

WHO SHE WAS

A nurse who had cared for Mama at our birth, I learned from Mama, had given me my name. "I didn't have a name and she said she wanted to name y'all so I said, okay." I had also learned early to not ask the obvious questions of Mama like, "Why would you not have a name for your precious baby girls?" Or, "Why you having another baby when we can't take care of us?" And, "Do you know that man who you just brought into our house?" Because asking any questions close to those got you slapped clear and clean across the room. So, to know that she had not considered at all what names to give us twin girls she had just birthed was left alone, just where it belonged.

That name I was given closely resembled my spirit and personified the Hebrew names of "Eva" or "Eve" to its full meaning, "living; enlivening." Except, in further research what was discovered was an "Ivvah" or Avva" whose meanings were much more disturbing.

One translation had those names' meanings being "overturned, ruined, and conquered" as in what happened to the city of the Assyrians. (2Kings18:34; 19:13; 17:24; 37:13; and Ezra 8:15). Deeper still, was the revelation of the meaning referring to "iniquity" and relating to one of two chief gods of Hamath, Arpad, and Sepharvaim. Then, too, even more troubling was the "Iva" or "Ahava of Ezra 8:15 who was a Babylonian god representing the sky; for them a sacred town.

Still, the greatest of all conflicts I would discover was as a Biblical reference the significance to my name had in the conflict that existed between two library cities (symbolizing both being repositories of great wisdom and knowledge) located on the sides of the great River Euphrates (symbolic of both having the life force of the word flowing through them). One library's name being a derivation of Ivah, Sippara (Sepharvaim), and the other, Anah (Hena); the former meaning "iniquity" and the latter, "troubler, or troubling."

These definitions would create the greatest conflict ever for the call that would be on my life. Gee, none of all this I had discovered was comforting. What I determined to do then, was to disprove all the negatives I had uncovered about me, or Iva's, supposed descriptors. I was not one who would be overturned, ruined, or conquered. Most of all, from what I felt in my spirit, it could never be acceptable to me that I be identified as a "pagan city of worship" – or as "one given to iniquity," as that library city sitting on the one side of the River Euphrates. What it appeared I would be called to do would involve me clearing up just who I truly was. What would be the characteristics that would identify this Iva? I began to wonder just where it was that Nurse Claudette researched to come up with my name. There had to be something more to her choice of that name for me.

WHO HE WAS

I actually knew very little about Marshall's life. I had met his only sister and, although she was a little eccentric, nothing really stood out as troublesome about her. His friends were mostly those folks he worked with and his extended family in the likes of the cousin I worked with. What I would learn of who he, Marshall Shire, was would be someone whose very name had a Biblically historical and spiritual connection to Queen Vashti's story. It was when I looked into the Queen's husband's name, Ahasuerus, or Xerxes, whether those were his titles or actual names some commentaries argue and disagree, I discovered the meaning "martial" and "ruler of heroes" or modern-day "Shah" as in Shah of Iran. It stood for the title given a "king." In addition, "Shir" referred more to the disposition of that king being as a lion. When put together, the title "lion king" was such a one as Vashti's King Ahasuerus who reigned in a line of ruthless, depraved, indifferent, and cruel kings of Persia.

I would come to realize that there was indeed a God-Plan for me marrying this man, Marshall Shire. The fullness of the assignment would not become fully revealed to me until much, much later into our marriage. There was something inside of me that I was being called to bring into our union that would cause my husband to change from the man he was to the one yet to be discovered. He was to give up and let go of his depraved and indifferent mindset and become a different kinder, gentler man.

What my overactive mind told me about Marshall instead, as I attempted to size him up, was that he was an educated, cultured, white-collar upper-management professional. Someone who all the young women I knew of in my age range were looking to score. What Marshall turned out to be though, was something so very different. He had barely finished high school and immediately enlisted in the service. His level of participating in cultural activities was to watch whatever the latest horror film was showing at the movies.

Then there was the partying every night, all night, after work. He would make his way to his favorite bar and get "head-swirling and turning" drunk. He said he was "unwinding" and in the mornings, he would be bright-eyed and bushy-tailed – like nothing had happened. There was a name for that condition I would later discover. However, for then, it was the normal lifestyle for many of the up and coming professionals in his age group and sphere.

With all those vices, it was easy to place all the blame for my not accomplishing my goals on Marshall. It was he, after all, who had resisted my evolving and attaining my life's hopes and aspirations. He had placed such ridiculous obstacles in my path. Obstacles like him not wanting me out of the house during the daytime to attend classes and insisting I be at home in the evenings when he got in from work. That meant no evening courses either. Therefore, none during daylight and none at night - it would have been great if there had been online courses in the mid-1970's. But there were not.

Then, when I had defied him and enrolled in courses anyway, my husband insisted, I not begin my homework until after our dinner and after watching whatever television program he feigned we had to watch together. There was a name for that type control over another I would learn about later as well. I could psych myself up that I would have enough energy to complete assignments after preparing our evening meals, serving him his dinner, and cleaning up after and putting away any leftovers.

Amazingly, I did make it to that point many nights, until the weight of it all overcame me. Had I been allowed, or "permitted" to exercise after our dinners, maybe the overwhelming "i-tus" would not have overtaken me. But either because of his sincere concern that we were in an unfamiliar place and he wanted to "insure my safety," I was not "allowed" go out after dark. Not permitted to walk around our gated community condominium complex in the Southside Bay Meadows area of Jacksonville. As I think about that location of our first home, it reminds me of how Fort Knox secure it was. Looking back still more, it was all such foolishness and stupidity – on both our parts- his for making it and mine for putting up with it.

Nevertheless, there in that strange new city with no one to confide in and separated from all my family and friends, my pride would not allow me to share such silliness with anyone. I would learn to hold in my rage and anger until...

Of course I felt Marshall was fully responsible, it was so simple to accuse him. I was being all I knew to be of an obedient wife and thought that his role was to, if not to help me to attain my dreams and goals, then certainly not to be the major driving force to hinder me from fulfilling them myself. I could not quite process how other women could tell me that they would have never, ever allowed a man to stop them from accomplishing their goals, hopes, dreams and aspirations; whatever it was they set their hearts and minds to.

They had no idea of what it had taken for me to get to the place from where I had come from. The odds of my being married to someone like him as opposed to being on the street tricking, or stuck with three or four babies, or strung out on some drug were overwhelmingly against me. So, I went from my Plan A, to Plan B.

Marshall was a well-groomed, well-dressed, Billy Dee Williams-handsome type. Though I could see signs of his insecurities in certain areas of his life, he masked them with a brutally bold and loud brashness when voicing his displeasure or demands. That is how I, at twenty-two, described his controlling and dominating – bordering abusive -- spirit. It was "cute" and "touching" to me when, as we were dating, he would always want – or more accurately, insist – on knowing where I was, with whom and what we were doing -- down to the smallest detail. What love-starved, emotionally needy, and unfulfilled young woman wouldn't run into such a relationship, falling headfirst?

Marshall had a committed work ethic and was a loyal long-time employee, full of potential, yet not eager to learn and grow. His spare time was spent partying and telling and playing practical jokes. By all accounts, he was outwardly friendly and likeable. There was a secret streak of evil to him she would get to learn more of.

The man she married was the third and youngest child of his parents who -- surprisingly were fourteen years apart in age - - the same as she and Marshall were. His father was a

United States serviceman, and so had Marshall been. The oldest of his siblings was a brother and then there was his sister between the two of them. At the age of one, Marshall's mother died from choking on her dinner. His father was said to have been there when it happened, but was not able to save her. It would be his father's mother who would care for the three of them after that. All went well for him until at the age of ten, his grandmother, who had given him such love and care since he had been the youngest and not-yet-weaned baby, also died.

It was then that their father's sister took charge of them, for a price that is. They could always tell if she was getting her payment for caring for them by how they were treated. Based on that aspect alone, they learned that their dad was horrible at honoring his commitment to her. She was the absolute worst. Their beatings were often and non-provoked. She spoke to them in language worse than any of the sailors in their tourist and Naval Base city of Key West. That aunt was mean.

The one redeeming feature about life with that aunt was that it came to an abrupt end - - she just up and left them. She moved to California leaving the three of them behind. That is where they all remained in that two-bedroom apartment fending for themselves. Their dad was years into another marriage with four new children and a wife who did not care for these other kids at all.

It would be a gross understatement to say that Marshall would grow and develop difficulties and issues with all his intimate and   interpersonal relationship and communication skills. His would be of the magnitude of a Depraved and Indifferent

Psychological Affective Disorder Type. She would get to learn all about that later, too.

THE GREAT PRETENDER

My chance encounter with Nurse Claudette would happen much after my marriage had been in full swing for years. So, what I had convinced myself of at this point where I was in life now, was that the only option left for me to take was to play the make-believe game of being the woman I so desperately desired to be. A woman who had not endured pre-birth and adolescent years of the trauma of abandonment and rejection. A woman who had grown up with two loving parents who had nurtured, trained, and protected her from all of life's evils and hardships. A woman who had accomplished all her educational and career goals and had been found by a man who with a deep abiding and everlasting love, married her; cherished and adored her and their children. When she walked into a room, her presence would be felt without a word being spoken. Her very persona would exude confidence and assurance. Yet, if they only knew the truth.

I would become a consummate "great pretender." Fearing that either I did not deserve, or I would never get to that place of personal fulfillment and accomplishment. Therefore, if I built walls around myself, I would keep under wraps the reality of who I truly was. Trouble with all that was, the walls got so thick that I lost the ability to connect – with anyone. I now feared being forever lost, even to myself. What it was all along that I really wanted to do was to let my hair down and experience those lost years of my unfulfilled youth.

I wanted desperately to be that inquisitive little girl; that exploring teen; and that fun-loving young adult who would evolve and transform into that perceptive and matured woman who had discovered her world and found all its great treasures. There was a place that one was to get to should they actually become such a woman, all self-assured and self-confident, poised and competent. None of those things had happened to me by now as I recovered from my time of physical, emotional, and psychological disorders and ailments. So for now though, I chose to fake it until I made it. I would give the appearance of having successfully evolved into that socially adept and emotionally well-balanced woman. Hoping all along that no one would find me out, unmask and uncover the "real me" of who I truly was.

So the ones complimenting me now, 'You can't possibly be fifty-two' never realized and knew nothing of, the struggle it took for me to face them and my world each day – a struggle of wearing the mask of the woman I longed desperately to be. All the while hoping I was fooling that world and that someday, I could pull off my mask to reveal the real me. Then, finally, my struggle to live just one more day through the weight of the mounting disappointments and fears and sensing that I might never, ever be who I was meant to be. Could I face and accept that woman? I hoped with all my heart for the time when it would not be so difficult facing my day-to-day life struggles. What was surprising is that many of them, God had brought me through as only he could – miraculously!

I had overcome the years of unrequited physical and emotional fulfillment during my marriage. I had lived through my husband choosing, after twenty-five years of marriage, to replace me. I actually thought his choice of a replacement was a very good one on his part when objectively evaluating her.

What she turned out to be was actually a twenty-year younger rendition of myself. She was attractive and appeared to have life by the horns. How smart of him. I couldn't help but think if he would do the same thing to her as he had with me. Would he resent her fulfilling her life's goals and dreams to become an accomplished and productive accompaniment to their team? Or, would he do the silliest of things to keep her from enrolling in courses, and then from studying for her assignments when she did go against him. Oh, I was re-living the pain. Let me pull up and "Wooosaaah!"

I actually hoped for her sake that she was stronger than I had been. I could only imagine though. I even confronted her at one point to let her know, "I am okay with you and my husband being together. But I just can't agree to my children and I being left penniless." What it took for me to approach her then was nothing short of the Lord God guiding me by his truth and love.

Struggles and trials continued with assaults to my children's futures and well-being. One would be entangled in never-ending legal battles. Another child would become the mother to our first grandchild while she was still a teenager and I would agree to place my life's goals, hopes, and dreams on hold yet again to care for that grandchild while our daughter finished high school and college. In the midst of these trials is when my husband would pass and some three years later, I would have to abandon our home of twenty-six years and encounter resulting financial challenges and struggles.

Having endured all those life experiences, the struggles and trials, along with the attacks to my health and sanity, I was now resigned to merely graciously accept the compliments of those who never really knew my full and complete story. Although it seems my inner me tried and tried desperately so many times to disclose to whoever would listen – the sad pieces of that story. Their words spoken in admiration of a woman they saw and accepted at face value would possibly have been so very different.

I secretly looked forward to when I could claim not only a restored life, but also full and complete restoration to my body, mind, and spirit. This would include all other aspects of my physical, emotional, and psychological health and wellbeing. What became most important to me, and what I most needed and looked forward to, was that I would receive spiritual strengthening and restoration. And I felt I had truly been on my way to that place, too. Those months just before I met -- my husband.

MEETING MARSHALL – MAKING PLANS

At the age of nearly twenty and acting much more mature than those young years, I was at a place of getting comfortable with the pain-filled, troublesome, and deprived childhood I had endured. I was looking forward to the new "me," I was hoping to become. It was the spring of 1974 and I was at a place of hopefully developing into a young woman who was free to explore life. I was employed in a position of authority and high regard within the local government of our large metropolitan city and my youthful and almost manic energy level allowed me to excel in that administrative support position.

I had begun to develop relationships and friendships with women, many much older than myself, who would become my mentors and life coaches. Finally, I was able to interact and communicate on a social level that allowed me to express myself freely and openly, and receive feedback on what was acceptable and what was not.

That administrative position also allowed me to experience the hierarchical needs we all have as humans to be met and many times exceeded. Most notable were my sense of self-esteem and need to be in control; and that I was earning an income that met and exceeded the needs of a twenty year old; and the emotional fulfillment and satisfaction I received from my many admirers. Though I did not have one main boyfriend, I considered all my admirers special. That soon would all change once Marshall was introduced into my life.

His cousin, who was an employee in one of the departments my boss managed, brought us together. I learned much later that this cousin of his was herself more than twenty years into the most abusive and egregious marriage that ever was. Talk about misery loving company. That cousin had told me one day, "You need to be married. That's what's wrong with you. And I know the perfect person."

It wasn't that his cousin had observed me to have loose morals or to be promiscuous. What had made her take notice was the exact opposite. Therefore, thinking that I could "straighten out her cousin" is why she wanted the two of us to meet. That my life just two years before would have looked sadly very different, albeit thanks to a redeeming God, that cousin's observation and consideration would have been quite the opposite.

What she was able to witness now was my energetic personality, knowledgeable intelligence, confidence, and outspokenness. Thanks or, no thanks to my fear of rejection, I didn't take any wooden nickels from anyone as I performed my duties as the County Recorder's Administrative Assistant.

Many of the women would remark that I was young, gifted, talented, smart, and, as they liked to say, "As cute as I could be." Because I was super-friendly and engaging, I was never considered a threat or envied by the other female employees. Though they couldn't seem to quite make out, or accept where it was that I said I was from. Although I told them time and again it was from not too far just up the road, Fort Lauderdale. They didn't quite believe me. I didn't talk like any of them or act like anyone from these South Florida parts. I was very different and if they knew how much effort it had taken

47

for me to not duplicate the lifestyles I grew up around, they would have understood.

That cousin of Marshall's must have thought I would be a come-up for him -- and I was. Only thing, though, Marshall would not be able to handle my 'coming up.' He asked me out to lunch that day we had first been introduced and we would have many, many more lunch and dinner dates before he asked me out to the movies. We began dating that first movie date night. It would be months later still that we would become intimate. I never fully understood why but was relieved that he wasn't all over me like most men I dated and had to fight off.

"So, you don't have a boyfriend, huh? He had asked me. "Nope, I don't" "Well. I want to keep it that way." Hmm, I smelled trouble a brewing and didn't know quite where it was going. He continued, "I don't want you to see anyone else."

"What do you mean?" Was my response. "That would mean that you and I were boyfriend and girlfriend. We would be in an exclusive relationship." He pondered the thought for a minute and said, "I guess so."

Wow! My first real boyfriend. A mature man with a white-color management position and the potential to be my husband! I was jumping up and down all inside myself.

Marshall had told me when he found out he was being transferred to a new city, still in the south but more north, "I want you to come with me."

But I let him know quick, "You want me to leave my job, my apartment, and my family to follow you?" I had not heard those words every female desired. So my immediate response to him was, "No. I don't think so." When he had added,

"I guess we can get married first." Spoken with all the enthusiasm of a dead fish. That was not the kind of proposal for marriage I ever expected to hear. So I told him again, "No, I pass."

Somehow, I knew I was more of a catch and so I did not intend to settle for less than first place in the life of whoever it was I chose to settle down with. I needed this man to understand some things about me before I undertook what was to be the greatest step in life for a young woman.

"There are things I want to accomplish in life before I get married. I want to finish school, start my career, and then have a family."

He said, "That sounds good. I want you to do that. I want the same thing for you."

I couldn't believe I was hearing his words. "Okay then," I continued. "Let's talk about what we each expect and we'll see."

The conversation later on was too surreal but at that time in my life, I wasn't smart or wise enough to catch on. I didn't know to trust my instincts. I had said, "Well, I want four children." He said, "Me too." "I want two girls and two boys," I added. "If any are twins, 'cause the chances are good for me having a set since I am one myself are good, then I hope they come first or second." He said, "Me too."

"I want them to have all the things they need to be successful and prosperous children and young people. Not 'play' things, but things to make them smart and interesting young people." He said, "Me too."

49

"And I want a nice house with nice things in it. Not expensive, but matching and clean." She recalled growing up in the tiny two-bedroom apartment, the only ones in town her single-parent mom could afford. Most times, they did not have furniture at all, and then other times it was whatever was being shared and donated from some agency. Wherever it came from, nothing ever matched. He was about to say it again, but she had caught on by now.

"No. You not going to just keep saying, "Me too" after I lay out what it is I want. You have got to have some things that you are expecting and I need to know what they are."

"Whatever it is you want. That's what I want too," he covered himself.

This wasn't right. Not just because that's not the way they did it in the movies and on TV, but also because I wasn't getting any idea of what was in his heart. What it was that was important to him. Something within her wanted to shout, "No! Don't fall for this! Get out of this mess and fast!" That's what she heard from deep inside of her. But what she second-guessed herself with was, "Here's a chance to make a life for the both of you that is outstanding and like nothing either of you have ever dreamed of. He's actually asking you to join him in it. No, he may not know how to express what he wants, but he's asking you to be with him." And that's all it took. Therefore, as he made plans to be transferred to the new city, I made the plans for our wedding.

THEIR WEDDING DAY

On "that" day, of her wedding to Marshal, her head was in such throbbing agony that even her eyes pained her. She had thrown up several times already and still felt like there was more to come. What she had learned through all these years was that something was about to happen and it was not going to go right at all. She knew she should put a stop to this fiasco, but how. The plans had been made for a long time and all she had to do now was to put on her dress and meet him down at the bottom of those stairs.

Why was she feeling so screwed up today? There were signs and "things" about Marshall she had discovered, which caused her great concern and seriously unsettled her. Try as she might to discredit her feelings, nothing worked. The reality of those troubling emotions was being experienced in every part of her body. Although she had told herself she would "learn to love him," she was not feeling him in any way at all right now – and on her wedding day. That sounded absurd. Wasn't this the way life was supposed to progress if she was the kind of young woman who kept to the higher standard? She had managed to keep herself from the lifestyle where it was she had been raised and that was a monumental accomplishment. How could she be besieged by such emotional and physical pains and discomforts? What was it her body and mind was desperately trying to warn her of?

Hadn't everything fallen into place? So why was it she was here now and ready to say "I do" to the man who'd asked her to be his wife; or at least first asked her to move in with him to the new city he was being transferred to. At least that told her he wanted her with him. At least. But, she knew better in her heart of hearts. She knew not to continue with this wedding. However, she could not do what was necessary to call it off. She could perceive that there was something even greater that was not right about Marshall -- but could not say what that was.

Never had all her senses been so piqued that every possible sensation she could experience was operating in overdrive. Her head was splitting. Her eyes were bulging and unable to focus on anything. It wasn't working very well, but keeping them closed felt best. Then too, how was she to apply her makeup and get dressed. Her stomach was so unsettled she dared not eat anything. Moreover, her entire body shook uncontrollably. If all that was happening to Vashti physically didn't convince her to not go through with this marriage, nothing else could. All her friends, family, and co-workers thought that she and Marshal were the perfectly matched couple. Nothing could be done to convince them otherwise, or be said to convince them this time, that what they thought was a perfect match, was as far away from the truth as could be.

There was supposed to be some semblance of solace for her to the fact that he was fourteen years older than her twenty-two years. She had secretly hoped that with his age would come a maturity that would blot out the years of adversities and challenges of the childhood she had endured that was fraught with pains of abuse, neglect and the absence of a loving male figure. It was hoped that his maturity would enable their lives to now somehow make up for all those years from the effects of poor single mother parenting. What she discovered though, was that his seeming "easy-going" and "carefree" lifestyle belied his true age – and even more his own troublesome childhood. She would later, albeit much too late to rectify, discover what allowed him to appear so carefree and happy.

After their wedding, they would move and live in another city, over three hundred miles away from her family and friends. They would live more than six years here where he had been reassigned. It was in this new city, in their new townhome, with her new car and all the trappings of convenience and leisure that she continued to realize what a great mistake had been made. Only thing now she was miles and miles away from being able to call anyone to come to her rescue. She had left everything and most importantly, her wonderful position. It would take her some time to get accustomed to this place and then to begin interviewing for another job.

DAYS OF DETERMINATION

It would be twenty years later into our problematic and troublesome marriage that the façade would all begin to fall apart. That point where I had made the decision and determined to make changes to my life – with or without Marshall's help. I would always wonder if it were my life-enhancing decision that opened the door for his actions.

Was it that I had finally gotten so fed up with my lack of personal fulfillment that he finally believed me and was prompted to begin demanding I "leave" and "just go?" That man had to know I would refuse to comply. I had given special efforts to making sure all appeared, on the surface at least, to be going along in our family as normal as usual and expected. I didn't let on about all I had been planning since deciding to go back to school to complete my degree. After all, this was long after and years since I had gotten over the fact that he resisted and resented me doing so. Even to the point of him saying, "You know you would have left me if I hadn't tried to stop you and put those obstacles in your way years ago."

My only response to him was, "Well, you know what? That is just what I am going to do, now. I am going to get my degree, get a position, start a career finally, and me and my children, we are outta here. You only delayed the inevitable for more than twenty years." I was refusing to stay dumb and ignorant allowing my intelligence to be used only whenever it was he requested it or felt it appropriate – and that was always whenever any matters of family business were involved.

I was the one called to interact with the professionals, transact business affairs, and then interpret for my husband what it was that had just transpired. If for any reason, the particulars of the transaction did not meet with his full approval or he did not understand, it was always my fault. I was always the one held to blame. Marshall never would agree to pray first about the transactions or seek counsel himself as the man of our home. The weight and the burden were far too much for me to continue to carry alone anymore.

VASHTI'ED

Of course, I said nothing that day when he finally revealed that his intent years ago had purposefully been to prevent me from completing and obtaining my degree. So, my response to him was spoken under my breath. I could not give my secret "I'm getting outta here" plan away - not until everything fell into place. Everything falling into place was my completing that degree, saving enough money to move out into a place of my own, and having a job with income enough to support myself and my four children. Until then, there I was – stuck, until... It was now that I was being told to "leave" and not take a thing with me.

Was it because of my refusal to continue to be a shield for his unwillingness or inability to learn to be the front man for our family? On the other hand, was it that I had taken charge of my life and began attending school again? There wasn't much else different going on in our lives so it must have been one of those two things that put me in a place of disobedience and rebellion.

What I was being requested to do differed from what Queen Vashti had been summoned to do? To "...appear before the king wearing her royal crown..." (It was implied "...wearing her crown "only..."). However, it would be my same response as that queen's had been, to refuse, that got me in my state of rebelliousness and disobedience. Queen Vashti had refused to comply based on the dictates of whatever the culture and societal norms of her times were.

In addition, for that queen, due again to the nature of the times she lived in, she would have been physically removed from her place, her home, the palace. In contrast, I would have to willingly let go and remove myself in order to comply with "Leave," and "Let go." I would have to be willing to forfeit all that I had endured throughout the past twenty years and just walk away from it all with nothing to show for those years' accomplishments or acquisitions.

Just as Queen Vashti must have been going about her every day activities and doing what a queen was expected to do; so had I been. Actually, I was even going above and beyond what was expected of me as a wife and mother. If my family only knew the extent, to which I had allowed myself to be humiliated for the sake of keeping in my husband's good graces. Marshall had a way of belittling and humiliating me that cut me to my core. I had not developed that tough exterior that others usually formed to protect themselves, even though growing up with older sisters who had not always been that kind and gentle to me and my twin.

Marshall knew how to hurt me deep down to my core, he seemed to delight in doing so -- and it did not take much for him to get started. The look on his face as I struggled unsuccessfully to hold in my tears was torturous. He sadistically enjoyed it and that fact made the pain for me all the more hurtful.

Of all that had happened to Queen Vashti - - losing her marriage, her position of esteem and honor, the material, financial rewards and benefits of being "queen" to the then most influential and wealthiest of world rulers; was about to be repeated in my life. Well, aside from Marshall being an influential and wealthy man anywhere near the likes of King

Ahasuerus, of course. The loss of relationships and attacks in the areas of my physical and emotional health -- all that and more was now about to come upon me, as well. My life experiences were about to practically mirror those of Queen Vashti.

So, it was at the time that I was reading and re-reading that Old Testament Book of Esther that I first began to realize the stark similarities in the queen's and my circumstances. I would learn of her dethroning and realize that the timing of my gaining this knowledge was coinciding with that of Marshall presenting me with his request. Well, that was actually putting it rather mildly. What he actually did was to demand that I leave and let go of everything.

Our situation's similarities were as clear and as obvious as the nose on my face. Even my name was there and hidden in that rejected woman's sad story. Moreover, due to my super-sensitivity to the comments and reactions of others, I was convinced they could see it, too. Queen Vashti's "they," were those who were the king's contemporaries who gave him the counsel to "put her away. My "they," were my children, my family (and because of my heightened sense of paranoia), the many artists, radio, TV, and high-profile entertainment, religious and secular personalities who were writing and singing songs about me, my situation and my "dreams and visions." My life was being played out in their sermons, song lyrics, plays, and movie story lines.

I could not imagine that something like refusing to leave a home, a lifestyle, the amenities and comforts of this world, the security of retirement investments saved over the years; all those things, I was to simply walk away from. It was never about holding on to my husband that I refused. It was never about my fighting for his love and devotion. Marshall's heart had never really been united with mine. He was a free agent and could leave whenever he chose, "Whom the Son sets free, is free indeed" (John 8:36) is what I would always tell him. No, I wasn't a queen, but I had definitely gotten myself entangled into one royal mess. Yes, I was feeling I had been wronged. In addition, yes, there was something inherent to my nature that would not allow me to acquiesce to what I knew to be a gross misrepresentation, disservice, and untruth.

It was all those years of having lived in my marriage and not living the truth and fullness of my giftedness that caused me the most hurt. I had shut down my sensitivity to it feeling it served no purpose for the times I was in. I had even accepted my name's meaning as "one who sheds light, discloses and reveals" because that is exactly how its character and personality traits had manifested and played themselves out all my life.

Situations or relationships I would enter into and either something I would say or do would have everyone scampering for shelter from what the words I had spoken would cause to be revealed and made perfectly plain and clear to everybody. It was at this very time, too, when I felt I was being Vashti'ed, that the realization of why it was I had such a problem with Marshall's demand became crystal clear. Only God and I would know the whole story.

That's what it was like in my first marriage to Marshall Shire, my "Xerxes." And it was that marriage that had nearly wore me completely ragged. I had been made to take control of each one of our family's affairs making all the decisions – great and small. I never considered there was a mental or emotional deficit component attached to Marshall forcing me into those situations. What could it have been that had him so terrified of interacting with authority figures so much so that he had me, a woman, and running interference for situations he should have taken control of? I had even been labeled "Jezebel" for doing what it was my husband had demanded and insisted I do. When I finally discovered what that term actually meant, I wholeheartedly agreed with them. Made for quite a conundrum. If they only knew the truth, it was he, who was forcing me into those take-charge situations repeatedly, "You're good with talking with people and figuring out what's going on.

You handle it."

Even when I confided to him that I felt too uncomfortable being the one going head to head with attorneys, real estate brokers, insurance agents, and other professionals, it never meant him no never mind. He still refused to take the lead. What did result from my being pushed into all those positions was that I acquired the knowledge and ability to help and assist my neighbors, friends and family with legal matters I would have never been privileged to know or understand. It was at the age of twenty-two that I in essence began to be mentored by all sorts of professionals who did not count it robbery to share their insight and wisdom with someone so young and inquisitive. So, though it may have been meant by Marshall to harm me, it all turned out for my good. And, that was all in the past, old stuff and "back then." I was embarking on a totally new beginning and phase at this season of my life. My "now" journey was about to begin.

A NOW JOURNEY

So, though they were all writing, singing about, or acting out what they understood of my life experiences, none of them could ever know my whole story. No, it didn't help that I had used every social media platform to let the world know what was going on with me. I wrote letters and created internet websites. They wouldn't understand unless they looked at everything, all my dreams and visions, their full and complete interpretations, and the special anointing that there was upon me that would render the greatest insight. Even I did not grasp the fullness of the impact and implications. Somehow, though, God would allow me to recall each one of those dreams and visions.

Unfortunate for me, in my times of spiritual immaturity, when seeking an understanding ear, I would indiscriminately share what God had given me. I must have seemed some kind of strange to all those who gave me a "You had a dozen eggs in your basket, but clearly several have cracked," look. Must have appeared some kind of strange to them all. Nevertheless, God and she knew different.

What I had done was to write them, the visions and dreams, all down in my journals, eventually typing them all into computer files. It was a wonder I still had them too. In all the packing and unpacking, moving and storing, that had happened to me. It was a miracle those journals and files from the desktop and laptop computers I had used throughout the years yet survived. Although at one point, the tablet journals somehow mysteriously went missing along with many of the computers and laptops.

Some had hard-drive crashes. Still others were outright stolen. Some of them would become infested and infected with viruses after Marshall and his "friends" had asked to use them. I did not know enough about technology at that time to realize what was going on. But eventually I caught on and restricted their using my computers at all. It was a principle learned years before to use every adversity as an opportunity to learn. So, this experience taught me the lesson of being acquainted with computer data security.

The practice of always saving your work was learned in the worst way when, as a legal secretary inputting a contract into my firm's newly purchased computer system. There was a key to save all and a key to delete everything. In a second, I was distracted, and pressed the key deleting and erasing forever all of the twenty-seven pages of that fifty-page legal-sized, single-spaced document. So, at the time I was writing my memoirs and documenting for posterity my life's experiences expressed in poems and songs, I had learned to put those works on zip drives and external hard drives for safety. That is where I would retrieve the Visions.

THE VISION SPEAKS - HER CALL

*"The sacrifices of God are a broken spirit
and a contrite heart..."*
(Isaiah 61:1)

*Hear my heart in these writings, Lord. Although the greatest pain
I've ever felt in all my life, I have endeavored to let my true heart
feelings be seasoned by your Word and therefore, ask that you
guide me accordingly.*

*No one is with her. She is alone and running down a
pitch-black dark and dusty, rock-filled road. There are potholes
and big and small boulders. It seemed to go on forever with no
end in sight. Tears are blinding her eyes and she is constantly
wiping them with her forearm. Those tears are combining with
the slimy, hot, thick fluid from her nose and are hindering her
breathing. There is a calming voice that she hears saying, "Stay
on the road. Do not turn back or turn to the left or the right. Do
not quit. You will make it. You will know when and where you are
to be."*

This scene has been with her for forever -- all
throughout her childhood but only more frequently and clearly
now in what some are calling should be her "fabulous fifties,"
her "fulfilled years." Years when, by no coincidence of The
Almighty, are the Gathering and Harvesting years for His
Chosen, The Church, The faithful, His Overcomers, The
Redeemed and the Called-Out Ones - those who are to rule and
reign in his Kingdom.

Only now did I connect my life's overwhelming
feelings of anxiety, apprehension, and uncertainty with that
scene. What was not clear was whether I was running from, or
to something. And when would those tears dry up? There was

never an end to the scene. It repeated over and over, again and again, never having an ending. It was just critically important that I keep running and not look to the left or the right. It was explicitly understood that I was under no circumstances to stop.

It was actually exhausting reliving that dream. My heart would pound in double time. I had even tried constructing my own ending when this dream came back. But sure enough, whenever it did, the exact same ending would happen – which was no ending at all. So, was this dream's increased frequency and timing associated with the gathering and harvesting of the redeemed and I had to get through some rough terrain and trying times to get my little tail in?

"For many are called and invited, but few are the ones to be chosen" (Matt 22:14)

Or, and more likely, was this a foretelling of the times I was about to go through. I would not see clearly the path. It would be full of hardships, rough and hazard-filled terrain. And for sure, I would be crying the whole time.

What people would not understand was that most of what I was experiencing in life was déjà vu and oh so surreal to me. That was a problem I would have to overcome – trying to get people to understand. God never told me at any time to "get the people to understand." Although He would, eventually tell me to "write the vision and make it plain..." It may have been sheer fear and trepidation; and if I were honest, the overwhelming magnitude of receiving and experiencing such unveiling and disclosing of dreams and visions for so many years. If folks had looked closely, they would have uncovered an even greater reason for me to stay the course, walk out the hardships and experiences I was undergoing and not give up or give in. There was a message, a storyline and a "purpose" to my every life circumstance and situation.

Problem for me was that they were of such an incomprehensible magnitude that someone like me was suffering to totally grasp it all. The final fulfillment would come at great cost and place an expensive toll on every aspect of my life. Many situations of my life would always remind me of that first dream that never, ever went away – or that never had a conclusion. What did finally become clear to me after all these years, was that its conclusion seemed to be determined by, and to be based solely on actions that I would chose to, or chose not to, take.

Should I endure to the end, there was a special gift that God had promised just for me. I would have to earn it. Moreover, it would take the strength of a walk of faith like none I could ever imagine. Even though I knew that I had been specially chosen, I would have to discover along the way what would be that great "prize" or special "gift" that God had just for me - - a woman who would survive the hardships, tests and trials she was yet to encounter. Whatever it was, she would have to pay a great price to earn it. No, it would not be in dollars, but everything else materially imaginable. It would not come cheap. It was I who would have to decide to stick it out or give it up.

It was a clue through a dream she received where names were being given to new babies. Their births had been beyond trying experiences for their mothers, but those little ones had eventually come forth. Some were given names according to

My testing would come during the time after Marshals' death. It was maybe five months later that I began to notice the opposite sex again. Nothing serious, but the idea of companionship and attention from a male was no longer repulsive to me. How I chose to answer would be the beginning of my journey. However, would it be the solution to my rebellion and disobedience as well?

LUST OF THE FLESH: GIVING UP AND SETTLING

When we are led purely by the flesh, we miss God completely. The Father was not permitting me to "settle" for what I felt would put an end to my so-called state of "rebellion" and "disobedience" by acquiescing to the first "proposal" offer I was presented with. At a time when I felt I did not wish to even begin to endure God's process, I allowed myself to become engaged to someone who was so very opposite of any man I had ever allowed myself to get to know, say nothing of even holding a conversation with, and let alone actually date. But, he was safe and he loved me "like an old man." The way he said that was between a threat and the most affectionate thing I had ever heard. It was like someone saying, "You belong to me" when you know full well those are the words of controlling and sadistic physical and mental abusers. Those are definitely not comforting words.

But my fiancé-to-be loved me with action. His love did things for me. He took care of those little and big things I had always had to do for myself with Marshall, but that all women look to a man to do for them. He ensured that my car was maintained and always full of gas. If anything in my place needed repairing or replacing, he made sure that it was done. He even shopped for outfits for me because he had noticed the kind of style I liked and wore down to the very colors that were my favorite. He was "all into me." There was absolutely nothing I wanted for. He even bought me a new car when mine needed only maintenance. And, when my master builder fiancé had begun spending time at a new job site that I didn't know the location of (he always told me everything that he would do during his early morning calls every day), it caused me to become a little suspicious and I found it suspect. It was way out of character and very unusual for him. He was the type to always voluntarily give an account of his whereabouts, leaving just the right amount of time in between, expecting me to reciprocate.

So, to my surprise, when he asked me to accompany him to that "secret" job location one day, it was to show me a beautiful five-bedroom estate home. He walked me through it asking what I thought about the different treatments and changes that were being proposed. He knew I loved home renovating and decorating, and was taking particular time to find out my feelings about intricate details to the remodeling of this house. He made me feel like a true queen. He had actually told me one day that it was his mission and number one job priority to find out everything about me so that he could be for me all that I needed a man to be. Whoa! That blew me all the way away! But God!

As we wandered throughout that house, I finally got it! It hit me like a ton of bricks, but I wouldn't and couldn't let on. I would let him go on thinking that he was just getting my input for whoever the "real" homeowners were. So, as he continued, "I told them it would be a good idea putting a fireplace there in that spot. But what do you think?"

That man made me smile, laugh, and feel so good about myself. His plan would be to surprise me with this house once we were married. He loved giving me surprises. I so treasured receiving his unplanned acts of kindness and love. If he had only known that his were the only ones I had ever received in my whole life from any man, including my dead husband Marshall, it would have given him even more joy when witnessing my responses. His love left nothing for me to desire - except...

I had heard young women bragging about their relationships with older men and how there was nothing on earth like it. Whew! I felt some kind of lucky at this point in my life to be experiencing one of my own, a "Girl, I'd have to hurt somebody – either you or myself - if you ever even thought about leaving me," relationship. But God! Unfortunately, try as I might to make it be so, this relationship was nowhere even close to God's Perfect, Divine Completion, and Will for my life. I had learned, and it was confirmed to me by His Word, that He, The Father, had a plan that far exceeded the superficialities of this world's material comforts and amenities.

It was as I busied myself one morning, that I heard a voice speak my name and ask, "Where are you?" I checked to see if there was anyone at the door or if I was hearing something from the television – but it was off. When it specifically repeated my name and asked again, even louder, "..., where are you?" I knew it to be that voice of God. The one I had heard from the vision where I was running down that road. I had gone to bed specifically with the intent of attempting to change that dream's outcome – just one more time. I was desperately trying to get it to fit my current circumstances – just where it was I found myself right now, so that I could put an end to it all. But it hadn't worked.

As I tried to force myself into that vision to possibly, turn the end of that dark road into the place I was now with my fiancé, that same voice called to me a third time, "Vashti, where are you?" And my little comedienne responded in Homer Simpson style, "D'oh!" I had no other answer to offer. "Not where you would have me, Lord. Forgive me. I'm so tired of it all. I need you to help me get back on track and to stay the course." I picked up my belongings and left. Never to return. I also left the ring and car keys. For I was still being prepared for that journey down a path I could not see clearly. God was going for something much bigger than even that amazing love I had felt from this master carpenter-builder with his grand surprises. I was in store for so much more than that overly generous fiancé could ever give to me. This would not be just about my wants, needs, and desires. And, yes, it would involve my special gift and ability to uncover and shed light on circumstances and situations. I had purposefully shut that part of myself down again because my fiancés religious beliefs neither accepted, nor tolerated such "gifts."

Learning that women were not even permitted to address their corporate bodies except in Bible Study or at times of open confession, left me feeling choked and voiceless. It would have been an extreme understatement to say that I was not deeply troubled. I, who thought I had something of such magnitude to say, found myself at a place where I had no voice at all.

"No, Lord. I am not where you would have me to be to fulfill your plan. If I believed the vision, it would be a plan that was to be tearful and heartbreaking, driving me so many times to my knees feeling I would be "brought nigh unto death itself." Would I be able to stick to the course even when life's situations and circumstances began to steal my very ability to get up every day? Trials like my son going through life-threatening battles with drug addition, facing years of imprisonment, and other of my children joined in relationships with people who my spirit felt were deceitful, perverse, and even demonic.

Even the trial of when it came to the time I had to leave the home we had owned for over twenty-three years. I somehow managed to pull myself together after each one of those situations to show to my children that I was "okay." Didn't matter that I had to visit the local hospital after each occurrence with elevated blood pressure and irregular heart palpitations. Would my health and sanity allow me to stick it out to the completion of this assignment?

I recall one such Emergency Room visit when the Triage nurse had performed an EKG. That Nurse had called over others of her co-workers to show to them my results. The attendant would ask me, "Are you sure you're okay?" "Except for my splitting headache, blurred vision, and dizziness," I responded sarcastically. "Sure, I'm just fine."

As I lay awaiting admittance into the hospital this time, I would overhear that nurse to say "...anyone with a reading like the one she has should have been pronounced long ago. And she surely should not still be functioning as she seems to be right now."

My God! At death's door, but God was keeping it shut. I would learn that it was God himself who opened the doors that no man could shut and shuts those doors that no man can open. (Revelation 3:7-8) Bless His holy name!

What could I do to prepare for such a testing then? It would have to be God Almighty who would teach, train, equip, direct and instruct me in what to do, say, and just how I was to walk through and walk out this thing I was being called to do. A totally new makeover would be needed. A "do over" of a life where so much effort had been put into shielding and protecting myself. So much had been covered up and buried in my life's hurts, pains, and disappointments - - and many of them self-inflicted, too. I had not escaped being molested and held deep-seated hatred and malice toward those who had perpetrated their violent acts and held even stronger feelings toward the ones I felt should have protected me. It even followed me into my marriage where, after six years, I had reached the end of my ability to tolerate its façade. Problem was now though, I had two little ones for whom I was responsible.

SEARCHING FOR LOVE
IN ALL THE WRONG PLACES

So, even though still married to Marshall, I was in desperate need of emotional and physical fulfillment. It was in the sixth year and the very same month we had our wedding ceremony, that I packed my two sons, our clothes, and a TV set into my little Toyota Tercel and left him, my home, and everything. Good thing for me child seats weren't the law back then 'cause my boys were packed in like sardines with all the stuff I had in that little car. I was 27 years old now and beginning to learn what it was I did not like or want to put up with. Unfortunately, what I did once I settled in my new location was to entertain a relationship that dishonored the sanctity of another woman's marriage.

Where I found myself now these thirty years later, with Marshall gone, and an engagement I had walked away from was again feeling the desperate need for physical and emotional companionship. Again, at that place where I had experienced great moral failing and it tore at my heart to think of doing the same thing again this time.

I could now feel what pain that woman suffered all those years ago at my hands and as a result of my actions. Actions, though committed in the ignorance and arrogance of my youth, yes; but actions that must have still brought to her gut- and heart-wrenching pain. My co-conspirator knew of the heaviness of the weight of what I'd caused his wife. It was he who, knowing that physical intimacy was at the height of what I was searching for at that point in my life - tried most eagerly to satisfy my seemingly unquenchable desires. However, he never did, and the weight of my actions – the late-night rendezvous and weekend getaways - was getting much too heavy to bear on my increasingly guilty conscience.

How was I ever to make it through whatever the tests, trials, and challenges I was to face to get to God's desired end? Yes, I earnestly desired to inherit His prize, greatest blessing, and promise. If only the guilt and shame of my faults, failings and multitude of my sins would allow me to. It would require a transformation and renewal of my mind from all I had experienced, conformed to, and known before. My mindset had been tested and I could now discern what it was that God desired - his good, and acceptable and perfect will. (Rom. 12:2)

CHAPTER TWO

TRANSFORMATION

We can rejoice, too, when we run into
problems and trials, for we know that
they help us develop endurance.
Romans 5:3

And be not conformed to this world: but be ye
transformed by the renewing of your mind, that
ye may prove what is that good, and acceptable,
and perfect, will of God.
Romans 12:2

A dilemma is a problem that can't be solved
without creating another problem.
Terry McMillan

DAYS OF PREPARATION

It would have to be a major life interruption on a colossal scope. Something of the grandest range and magnitude that would cause me to be open and willing to even entertain the idea. Imagine getting prepared to take on a mind-altering, life-changing, world-shifting challenge. What it actually took that caused me to get to that place of surrender and submission to God's Will was no less than a total major physical "shut down" and emotional "breakdown."

It was a "life interruption" of a grander than grand scope that affected all my physical, emotional, and psychological states and turned into a time of total "shut-in." It was my "Damascus road" experience and meeting time with the Lord. It happened on the twelfth day of January of 1997.

LIFE INTERRUPTION - HER "DAMASCUS ROAD" BREAKDOWN

While following my normal Sunday morning's routine, I had done the usual to prepare myself and gotten dressed first. Normal for me at the beginning of the month would be to either perm (touch-up or wash only), blow-dry, and style my hair. I would apply my makeup and then put on my clothes. Getting breakfast ready for the five other members of the family would be next. Our Sunday morning breakfasts were special to us and usually consisted of bacon and sausage, grits and eggs with either biscuits or toast. I got such pleasure in preparing meals for my family.

The boys always ate heartily and my only daughter was the fussy princess. Marshall had made coffee way before I got up and I would have a second cup while cooking. Sometimes his coffee tasted a lot different from normal. He would always bring my first cup while I was still in bed so; I attributed it tasting different to him not knowing exactly how much cream and sugar to used. His "act of love," in bringing me coffee, was so different from his normal selfish and self-absorbed "me first, last and always" personality.

After getting the four of our children out of bed and cleaned up, they all got dressed, fed, and we were on our way - - off to attend worship services. My children were always as eager to attend services as I was. Those kids amazed me at how diligent and enthusiastic they were to learn the Word and to follow God's ways. They would always pay extra special attention during the times of Bible Study I had with them at home. I was especially proud of their knowledge during the times our church families would meet for study as well. My children were always full of questions and eager to feed on The Word of God. It was so very different for me as a child. Not only did we not have a home Bible Study, but we rarely went to church at all. There were missionary groups who came into our apartment complex for Vacation Bible School. We treasured those times.

Our family's church congregation was a small one of folks with young children like ourselves and where we adults had more than one responsibility or duty. This wasn't the place where you were positioned according to your calling and giftedness. You had to 'git in where you fit in.' Among the many assignments I had was to sing on the Praise and Worship Team. It was after having sung that January 12 morning that as we were leaving the pulpit area, I suddenly experienced what felt like a vice grip enveloping and squeezing the front of my head.

It caused me to instantly fall to the floor as my head was gripped in excruciating pain. I sensed my body's temperature instantly spike to an unbearably high level and my blood pressure reading would be 200 over 160. Because the left side of my body was becoming fully paralyzed, I began with my one free right hand and arm, to peel out of all my clothes. Unconsciousness soon followed.

It would be weeks later that emotional and psychological issues would put me in a state where I was relegated to addressing only my most basic of daily needs. Because I needed to make connection with the outside world, I arranged a sleeping area in the bay window of the front bedroom my oldest son, now away at college, had occupied. Truth be told, that was the sleeping, reading, eating and "gazing out the window" area for the next three years of my life. Everything I needed was pretty much within arm's reach – my laptop, the TV, DVD, and stereo system.

My day-in-and-day-out routine became early morning first feeding on the Word of God. Then taking in food needed to feed, nourish, and sustain my physical body. Mid-morning and mid-afternoon naps would follow after breakfast and lunch so that I would give to my body and mind the time of rest and rejuvenation it required. This cycle was repeated over and over, for what must have lasted nearly three years. The TV stayed on either TBN or other stations that played the CSI, Criminal Intent or whatever other investigative crime shows. That which filled my day most was either reading the Word of

God or listening and watching the Word on DVD. My compromised mind was a sponge and the more I took in, the stronger I got.

I wasn't expected to live very long at all according to the physician's reports. Even I believed those reports of the doctors, psychologists, and other healthcare professionals. Until... Many friends and family were writing me off during this time as well feeling that I had completely "lost my mind" and was manifesting terminal, life-threatening health issues. It was nothing for me to visit the Emergency Room at least once a week. Most times, I would try to take myself for fear of causing panic in my children. It was most disturbing when I sometimes overheard my husband, Marshall confiding in phone conversations with persons unknown that, "She ain't got long. She acting and looking crazy and sick."

My younger set of children, a third son, and last-born only daughter, although petrified of their mother's physical and mental state, were at a loss as to how to respond. They were both entering their teen years and in desperate need of attention, love, and guidance from their parents. My hopes were that their father would provide and look after those needs of theirs - as any loving parent would under such circumstances. Of course, once again, I was wrong. As I would learn years later, they had been pretty much left to their own devices, and to fend for themselves.

In their earliest teen years, an overprotective and doting mother becoming so ill was the worst possible scenario for them. I would pray for God to heal them from the hurts, pains, and disappointments they were suffering during this time – and the resentment I would later learn they would build in their hearts towards me for being ill. Children at that age understood recovering from broken legs or arms; from operations to damaged or diseased organs, but conditions where there was no blood or scars was something they could not grasp. So they were angry – and at me.

The older of the first set of children, a son, didn't learn of the severity of his mother's state since I kept my status from him so as not to interfere with his studying while at college. I didn't need him carrying the burdens of my illness. The second-born son did all he could to help care for me. Nonetheless, it was too much of a huge burden to a young man looking after the day-to-day needs of an incapacitated mother and two younger siblings. He, too, was on a course to graduate from an accelerated academic high school program of study. I needed him released from this burden so that he could complete the dreams and hopes I had for his life and that he deserved.

There could not be a repeat of what happened to my dreams of completing college. They had been quenched and stymied even though I had been like my children, a promising and devoted student. So, despite being in my compromised state, I couldn't allow the same thing to happen to them.

I had sacrificed my Plan A of first completing my education, entering a career path, and then having children after four or five years into that career; for my Plan B. I would have my children first and then, hopefully, finish my education once the last of those children were in kindergarten. I was not about to allow any one of those children to miss their opportunity for success because of my illness. My firm intent was to insure that this second son stayed devoted solely to doing the very best that he could in his advanced classes. And that was not happening while he was trying his best to care for me and his younger sister and brother.

Therefore, with all the strength and energy I could muster for the times that that son was at home, I performed whatever duties I could to the best of ability. It meant that I literally fell out beyond exhaustion like a log at night, but I had to get him to see that I could do some things for myself. He was never really fooled though, and still insisted on chipping in to help me. It was when time came for him to go off to college that I had to have the "heart to heart" with him, insisting that he would not take time off to get a job to help support his brother, sister, and me. No way was I having that. He had to go off to college. He would still call back home several times during the day, though. That endeared him so much to me.

Because my illness had happened at the same time that my husband began to "invite" me to leave, my initial pleas were that God would end this time, cut it short and take me out of the pain and heartache I was experiencing. But, as it turned out, even I did not recognize or realize what God was doing in my life through that time of sickness. Until... as I delved deeper into His Word and prayed for His intervention into the overwhelmingly strong winds, earthquakes and fires of my situations, I began to hear Him answer me – ever so softly and clearly. (1Kings 19:10-14)

The Word became alive! It guided and directed me. It gave comfort and assurance. It healed me of all the diagnoses and prognostications from those speaking disease, destruction, and death over my life. God's Word was indeed alive and living on the inside of me. Moreover, the assurance for me now was that *I too was alive in him! I would live on! And I would thrive!*

I now felt equipped to take on the challenges of what I was about to endure. It was God's sovereign plan to have me to sit at Jesus' feet, take in, and taste of all the fullness of the meat of His Word. He desired I 'sup' on that Word morning, evening, and all throughout the day and night. I was to approach it as though it were the only thing that mattered in life – 'cause it was.

God's Plan took on even more clarity once my Marshall let it be known that he desired I leave "with just the clothes that I owned," and nothing more. Thing was, though, the Lord had shown me during my time of isolation and incubation in His Word that many things were, indeed, to happen to me - being asked to leave being one of them. God had forewarned me that I would not have to fight in that battle, though. The fight had already been won and it was God Almighty who was the Victor.

While still in my state of illness, and time of resting in the Lord, I had not kept up with what was going on in the world outside of my daily functions of managing and caring for myself and, as best I could, looking out for my children. I wasn't up on what was happening within any of the circles of people I had once associated with. In the spirit, though, I could hear of what kind of times we were experiencing. What I heard - more times than was comforting for me - was that in the times ahead, a more preferred, worthy, and deserving wife and "queen" was to come for those men who so desired. So, since it had already been revealed that my husband no longer found me to be his preferred, I began to hear more clearly the words of more voices directing me to do what I found incomprehensibly difficult to accept.

I resolved instead that I would rely upon my studying of God's Word and its directives. Once that mindset was adopted, it all became practical and clear to me. The Book specifically laid out what was to happen if a man was no longer pleased with his wife. Old Testament, true, but it directed that he was to "give her a writing of divorcement." Cool. I could accept that. Divorce me and go on with his life and me with mine. Considering all the other occasions where ending marriages or granting divorces were mentioned, I saw that the whole matter was based on the "heart conditions" of the men at this time. Seeing that was the case, then, my particular situation took on much more meaning for me – and other women going through like situations.

Because Jesus Christ came to show to God's people the heart conditions they were to have, then these men were to exhibit that "heart of Christ" regarding putting their wives away. But, as in my situation, that was not happening. The words I kept hearing repeated, without consideration for the wellbeing or welfare of that wife or those children was to "Just, let him go" and "Get out." "Leave." It was my initial response to give in, concede to what I was being told to do. Except...

There was a conflict between what God had shown me of His Word and what I was being instructed to do. I knew I was a new and different kind of woman -- not at all like those women in the times of the Old Testament - thank God. Many writers tell of how those women were not taught of the Word of God so they knew little to nothing of what this woman, I had learned. I was of a generation that had been enlightened by the Holy Word of God through the saving Grace and Mercy of the work of the shed blood on the cross by His Son, Jesus Christ. He had allowed us to develop personal relationships with Him for ourselves. We spoke and prayed to Him and He communicated through His Word with us. We knew Him for ourselves! It was man's doctrine and ways they were attempting to have me adhere to... not the sovereign Word of God through His Son Jesus Christ.

Even so, everything about the "old me" wanted to totally disregard all my "knowledge" and what I thought I "knew of the Word." I just wanted to say, "Yes. I will let go and leave." Except... the Spirit of God was letting me know that He had another plan and He would cover, shield, and protect me while I walked through it all. I didn't know why or for what purpose, only that He would eventually reveal both to me. I would be tested and tried in every way imaginable and it would be my refusal to accept anything less than God's Promised Divine Best for me that would cancel and nullify the test. His plan would have me in defiance of, and rebelling against my husband's decision and desires - ultimately opening me up for many heart-wrenching troubles.

What I felt too, was that my former lifestyle, before my marriage and during a time of separation from my husband, times when I committed acts of gross ignorance and arrogance, God would now test my sincerity, commitment, and faith. It

was in a vision that He promised me, my family, my children –
all of us – that "everything would be well - especially for the
younger two children." It seemed for those two all hell's forces
had been unleashed. I couldn't make a decision unless it
carried with it those guarantees of God's promises. I couldn't
walk into a situation "thinking" it was what God was calling me
to do only to find that it had been the deceitfulness of life - its
lusts and fleshly desires that I'd given in to.

God would be true indeed to keep His promise to
shield, cover, and protect me. Only if His Word had truly
penetrated my heart making me the new creation He desired –
and the person I would need to be to see His victory. So, as I
heeded God's Words and directives instead, my defiance and
rebellion would be the catalysts to start me on my VASHTI
journey. I would be stripped of all that I thought I owned – my
resources and finances. My relationships with my children and
family members would be estranged. The rejection and
abandonment – would attack my joy and all my life's hopes and
dreams. The lack of true intimacy and affection I had
experienced during my thirty years of marriage would be
nothing compared to finally being widowed, single and still
desiring intimacy in the worst way - only to have it yet
unrequited. Then, the disappointment of finding myself at a
place where all possible hope of things ever turning around
was fading. I felt for sure no one would, could - or even should,
ever love me again. Sad to say, this woman couldn't say I loved
myself at this time.

I was being called to forsake what I knew of the
world's ways of handling problems and challenges. God

wanted for me to be a living example, a testament, to His people of what He could do in a messed up, "tore up from the floor up" life that had been fully and completely devoted to Him. I would be making a journey from having rebelled against, and stood in defiant disobedience to, the accepted ways of society to a place of obedience and reliance on the Divine Purpose and Plan of the one true God.

Still, the questions abounded. What was it going to take for me to go through these processes? What exactly would those processes be? What would it take for me, and those I was thought to be rebelling against, to see the Divine Plan and Purpose God had for my life? Would I be able to endure those processes? Would I recognize His leading and guidance along the way? And, as important, how would I know when it was all over and ended? It was on a path that would usher in the promises God had made to me. What I now had to do was whatever it took to get to where it was I would be living the life of a woman who totally relied and depended upon her God.

"HER" NIGHT WITH THE KING

The timing of my husband's request was taking place during publicity releases for the movie about the deposed Queen Vashti. What a coincidence! It was in the years 1997 to 2000 that I was recovering from my stroke and would spend time in God's Word. Now five years after, there was an onslaught of multiple media advertisements for this movie. I had yet to learn of the spiritual connections, symbolisms and significance this movie's theme embodied for my life. There would even be an encounter with someone associated with the film that God would use to help me manage my way along His path to my restoration and deliverance.

I had caught the end of one commercial for "One Night With The King" and each time I watched it, there arose a deep, pain-filled aching in the recesses of my heart that totally engulfed me, buckling me to my knees and bringing on a torrent of tears. Tears that wouldn't - try as hard as I might, I couldn't stop. I knew exactly why it was that I was having such an intense reaction too. Those things going on in my marriage so mirrored what would happen in the story of the Book of Esther, the soon to be, newly chosen queen to King Xerses. "Things" that I was not emotionally able to yet process of the trials and tests my own marriage was experiencing.

True, I had been clearly made aware that I "no longer found favor with, nor pleased" my husband. Where I was in the process of all that now, was searching God's direction on what exactly I was to do, because it was clear that His Word was saying, "Stay." My study of Ecclesiastes 10:4 KJV, NIV, and NKJV) revealed:

If the spirit of the ruler rise up against thee, leave not thy place; for yielding pacifies great offences.

If a ruler's anger rises against you, do not leave your post; calmness can lay great offenses to rest.

If the spirit of the ruler rises against you, do not leave your post; for conciliation pacifies great offenses.

It was that verse and others, that even though I prayed hard to be released from the pain-filled goings-on and wanted desperately to hear God say, "Yes. You may freely leave and go," I only heard instead Him whisper to me,

"It was by my Permissive Will that I allowed you to endure the long years of this relationship. There were great testimonies you both were to tell of my grace and mercies throughout your entire lives. Then, because you had heard my voice when I confirmed to you that Marshall was not my Perfect Will for all you have been through during the years of your young life, you still persevered through the physical and emotional traumas of that day to take on the task. You agreed to my promise that I would be with you through it all if you would be to him what he needed to become the Man of God I desired he be."

"You stuck to that assignment my child, loving him when he was most unlovable. You sacrificed and submitted yourself looking forward to the reward for your faithfulness. So, then, Marshall never allowed himself to be fully humbled and submitted to my guidance and leading so that I would get the Glory for bringing him through his harsh life and into the many blessings he enjoyed in life. He instead chose to take for granted the wealth and comfort I allowed because of my goodness and favor towards him. It is now, that your reward is established, sure, and secure."

God continued, "No, you didn't get to have the life testimony of two people who had made it through the travesties, challenges, tragedies, and adversities of your lives. But I will still yet get the Glory. I still have a plan to bless your life's many sacrifices."

What God now desired of me, that He was reserving - should I choose to fulfill it – was a new assignment. He would give to me a special reward depending on whether I could successfully stay the course He would show and guide me through. There would be an unfailing devotion, commitment, faith, love and trust I would need to develop that would allow me to endure. Could I, and would I? Both questions were equally critically significant.

HER DETHRONING - "OH HELL/HAIL," THE QUEEN!?

Just one week shy of our thirtieth wedding anniversary in May of 2007 Marshall had died. I had been his caregiver and nursed him since discovering in the winter of 2005 that what he had called Irritable Bowel Syndrome was actually a stage four condition of something much more deadly. He was now gone and I was left to face mountains of challenges. I had been for Marshall a constant companion during his illness. That I had been able to be a loving and caring caretaker after enduring the pains of his request, was also a test for me. There were many days that he was non-ambulatory, unable to get himself out of bed at all - - days when he had undergone chemotherapy and radiation treatments or had a bad reaction to a change in his medications. I confess that I actually considered repaying him for the pain and heartache he had caused me. That time when I wanted to do all of the evil "Diary of A Mad Black Woman" things to him. But God had said to me on a day when Marshall was particularly vulnerable. "I still love Marshall. Even in his disobedience and refusal to obey me. The way you decide to treat my son, will be multiplied to you when you reach this stage of your life."

I resolved immediately that my husband would get only the very best care from me and all others looking after his needs. It was sad and such a waste of two lives that the covers could not be pulled back on the devastating life events the two of us had endured. The rejection and abandonment by those responsible for bringing us into this world; molestation, incest, rapes, abuse and misuse by family members and strange people invited into our lives. God had given us the ability to triumph in spite of all we had experienced and He wanted to get the glory – not our employers, or our intellect or anything anyone had done for us. Marshall was too busy "living the life" during our early years of marriage to take heed.

And then, in these final years, he was content to continue amassing wealth to spend with his "new bride." Therefore, the two of us never got to testify to God's faithfulness in bringing us out of our pasts and allowing us to live in the blessings and goodness of the lives we were now experiencing. Ours was a marriage lived under a total façade, like the many other couples who had aspired to reach the "middle class." I had learned that the material trappings of our lives could never satisfy the deeper yearnings of either of our souls. Marshall and I had not come to a meeting of the minds on that.

TWO LIVES INTERTWINE

So, now he was gone and the theater date for the showing of One Night With The King had finally come. I didn't have the courage to go see it alone and there wasn't anyone I was close enough to, or comfortable enough with, to ask to sit with me through it either. What I felt for sure, just based on my reactions to the Christian station previews, was that it would be an overwhelmingly emotional experience for me. And I was right. There were none of the actors in the film who particularly caught my attention. Sure, Omar Sharif and Peter O'Toole drew big box-office crowds in their day. The famed Tommy "Tiny" Lister as the eunuch, "Hegai," held some interest for me because of his "Long Green Mile" notoriety.

It was a totally different actor who I would not be familiar with, or take notice of at all - until later that year - who was to become instrumental in preparing me to fulfill God's plan and purpose for my life. Was it his face I had seen in my quiet time with the Lord? This co-conspirator of King Xerses' buddies who joined in counselling him to "handle his business" with his rebellious wife. For obvious reasons, I didn't take too kindly to his character. I could not yet translate that vision properly where a man's toothy smile was so bright that it glared a radiating glow of illuminating light. This would be the second of two visions of a man's face. That first face was of a short, stout-statured man whose smile was not so much from his teeth, but from the glare of metal from inside his mouth. That connection with my marriage to Marshall had been made and I understood who he was. But the association to this movie and the vision of a second man who had a toothy smile and who

94

would be associated with my marriage, did not connect yet for me at all.

So, I was left to ponder what exactly was to be the impact of this second vision and that one's involvement in my life's journey? Exactly what involvement would there be and how would he be associated with the plan God had for me? There was a gnawing feeling that the one God was using to speak into my spirit during this season of my life could possibly be that one. Surely, God was using his biting, often brutal messages to cause me to look at those areas of my life that were not yet submitted to the Father's Will. Words of conviction causing the greatest change and transformation in my heart. And, too, he did have that smile...

But, there I sat pondering those visions and watching that movie, alone, and all by my petrified self. Because of what I knew of the outcome of this Book of Esther, it wasn't only due to the fact that there was one heart-breaking scene after another that had me in tears. Neither did it escape me that the preservation of the entire Jewish race was God's plan in having Vashti deposed and replaced by Esther. It was just that I knew the devastating loss to be experienced by that poor woman – the very same as my life was experiencing and undergoing devastating losses. Yes, I sympathetically identified with one of the movie's protagonists, that defiant, rebellious Queen Vashti.

I had read and researched Vashti's story so many times years before – and several times after that so I had become more than too familiar with it. Even so, I always arrived at the same questions that I asked of my own situation, "Why would a loving husband (king) ask such a thing of a wife he supposedly treasured?" And, "What really happened to the Queen, Vashti?" I needed to know the answers sensing they would give me relief for my own outcome as well.

My earliest readings had me questioning and wondering why it was this queen was called to do something that was as much demeaning, abasing, and humiliating in those times as it would be for me today. Some commentaries had King Xerxes described as being in a wine-infused and boast-filled state when he sided with his advisors, who were indulging in "a drunken feast," and ordered his eunuchs to bring his beautiful Queen Vashti before him. "... *with the crown royal (only), to show the people and the princes her beauty: for she was fair to look on. But the Queen Vashti refused to come at the king's commandment by his chamberlains*": (Esther 1:11-12, KJV).

I could not wrap my mind around the mindset of such a request from a king who was supposed to love, cherish, and protect his queen. Why would anyone level-headed and clear-thinking cause his beloved to suffer such shame and humiliation? Well, if the accounts of his drunkenness were true, then the answer was sadly obvious. In further readings, the answer became much clearer still as I considered the God-ordained assignment of the young "Hadassah." She would be known by that term within her Jewish culture.

However, as she was being prepared for King Ahasuerus' harem, having been instructed to keep the fact of her Jewish heritage a secret, this young woman would be addressed by her Persian name, Esther. It was Esther who would become the one chosen to most "please the king and to find favor in his sight." Her bold and self-less actions would prove to save God's chosen people from annihilation. An act that way out-weighted Vashti maintaining any of her own personal concerns – her status, position, possessions, and livelihood; and yes, even her very life. That fact this one understood... but still.

Esther's character was nothing like that of Vashti's. But then, too, Esther had not had to endure, as research revealed, the years of the king's psychopathic personality – this fact was even intimated, and alluded to in the film. There was a level of depravity and indifference to his personal character that I would recognize in another – it would be exhibited again in the one who had the kings' same wanton disregard for other's welfare and emotions. Sure, Queen Vashti loved him, but everyone in his kingdom knew he was a bit "touched" and strange – much like my Marshall, who mirrored the king's personality. However, none of the people in King Ahasuerus' day and time, or in Marshall's, dared speak it aloud, or to the wrong persons.

So, on top of being made a queen at an early age, and silently enduring unspoken episodes of shame and humiliation from a king with demonstrated psychological issues, Vashti now had issues of anger, rejection, and abandonment. And, if the versions of the stories that had the queen executed were true, then the sheer thought of such an impending doom would have been more than she could physically handle. On the other hand, if she were either merely divorced and banished, never to appear before the king ever again, then she would have borne day in and day out, the pains from the consequences of her refusal to obey his request - - without there ever being any hope of resolution whatsoever.

Of the two possible consequences to Queen Vashti's gross defiance, my task of deciding how I would overcome the challenges before me were made two-fold. First off, I would have to keep myself alive if my death was the hoped-for outcome by watching out for any irregularities in anyone's behavior or any sudden change in the status of my many physical ailments, or through some other suspect method. And then, I had to find my way to getting my heart mended, realizing what havoc the acts of emotional and psychological assaults were causing to its condition. They were my double-duty emotions of empathy and sympathy for Vashti that were renewed all the more as I considered how too very similar the experiences we were encountering actually were. The parallel situations of betrayal, rejection, abandonment, shame, humiliation, and isolation.

Then, too, we were both to be marked for stripping of our inheritances and wealth, rejected by our spouses, dismissed from our positions, disinherited from our worldly possessions, and sent spiraling into calamities, catastrophes and life events never before imagined. I was certain these were the issues to be encountered, and what that Queen would begin to live out and must have gone through those so many hundreds of years before. It mattered not that this Vashti's specific circumstances, - seemingly very different due to the highly modernized, high-tech and mechanized information era I was now living in - still held gross similarities to those of King Xerxes' Vashti.

So, as I sat fixated on this movie, additional feelings of fear and anger engulfed me. Fear, for the stark and vivid similarities to my own story; and anger, because it did not have to be that way. As I watched the scenes unfold, I imagined all that Vashti must have been encountering and experiencing, banished and replaced by "...*another... better than she,*" (v. 19) the sheer agony of those thoughts kept me in torrential streams of those same tears from my earliest year's dream. I could sense my journey was really just beginning now from the intensity of my heart-throbbing, body-aching tearful sobs. No, those tears were nowhere near about to end. Still it didn't stop me from wondering just if and when they ever would.

Okay, it was all becoming clearer and in my reading and re-reading of the Book of Esther – I got it! I really did! I understood that God had a plan to rescue his people from annihilation and was using the two women. Using the older one whose personality was one of unyielding adherence to the established societal customs and norms, behavioral dynamics and rituals of her times. Dynamics, which were combined with a heightened sense of superiority and supremacy. And rightly so. After all, Vashti had gone through her time to be chosen from among so many other young women as "his most-desired" to her King Xerxes as well - and way before Esther came on the scene. It was she he had chosen at that time to be his "most special" from among the so many other beautiful young women. But now, unfortunately, it would be her inability to yield to and accommodate his harsh and insensitive request that would reveal her rebellious and defiant spirit, clearing the path and making the way for the wise and beautiful, albeit younger and oh so impulsive, Esther.

It would be Esther's spontaneity, beauty, and prudence that would be her winning attributes over all the other young virgins vying to replace Queen Vashti. Esther would be the one who, when it was her turn to go into the king, *"... required nothing but what the eunuch Hegai, the king's chamberlain and keeper of the women, appointed..."* (v. 15). Yeah. Yeah. Yeah. I knew, and finally fully accepted and understood that there was a much grander, greater plan and consideration for having Vashti replaced. But still...

I was so messed up watching this story unfold on the big screen by now, though, that by the time the carriage, which we are to believe contained Vashti, drove off to destinies unknown, the fluids from my eyes and nose were both running uncontrollably. It was difficult to understand why my tears and sobbing wouldn't subside. After all, it was a movie and a long ago story of a Bible character for goodness sake.

Somehow though, there had been a transference of every emotion of that woman into my heart and spirit – and they both were hurting bad. That had to be the something more, than me just simply being overcome by unexplainable, uncontrollable emotions. It was that I was one in mind, heart, and soul with the heart of Vashti. My thoughts and feelings were the same as hers. How could I ever recover from such a state? What would have to happen to free us both from this reproach and condemnation? The questions were for us both, for we were now one and the same.

CHAPTER THREE

CONFORMATION

And you will know that I am the LORD, for you have not
followed my decrees or kept my laws but have conformed
to the standards of the nations around you."
Ezek. 11:12 (NIV)

As obedient children, do not be conformed to the
former lusts *which were yours* in your ignorance,
1Peter 1:14 (NASB)

The woman who follows the crowd will
usually go no further than the crowd.
The woman who walks alone is likely to find
herself in places no one has ever been before.
Albert Einstein

HER ROAD BACK

It was my choice to believe that Vashti had indeed been merely banished and disinherited but would surely, one day, be restored. That woman would make the journey from wounded and broken to obtain and walk in full healing and restoration. Finding out exactly what it would take, the processes, procedures, channels, paths and courses she would have to take were just the beginning. She would undertake whatever was required of those processes in order to be made whole, so that maybe, just maybe one day, she could see the restoration and return of romance, relationships, finances, and all the world's comforts, to her life once again. Surely... Maybe... One day ...

That was the same road I would have to take to accomplish restoration for myself, too. It was one I never, ever would have volunteered for, or want to travel. Actually, I fought hard, at first, against many of the twists and turns. The battles to keep those things I knew I would have to eventually let go of; my home, our properties, the secret bank accounts, and our joint investment retirement accounts. It was a season where banks were repossessing homes and I would no longer have the income to maintain the mortgage payments and monthly home expenses. Also, because - at Marshall's insistence - we had mortgaged our home, not once, but twice. Once to make major repairs and then again to cover legal fees for a close family member, I knew for certain that where our family had lived for the past twenty-six years was marked for the foreclosure process.

Then, there were the ever-increasing stages and processes of rejection by once-close and dear friends and associates. I experienced abandonment by family members and even my own children, who desired to distance themselves from their "strange" mother. Those situations spawned a self-imposed isolation to protect my ever-growing and increasing aching heart and emotions. These things happening to me amid the accompanying whispers and stares were sometimes more than could be tolerated mentally or emotionally. Could I ever come to grips with any of it?

When crying and being miserable about those former friends' reactions to me became enough already, I simply -- stopped. God had promised to give me *"beauty for ashes, the oil of joy for mourning, and the garment of praise for the spirit of heaviness"* (Isa 63:3). Now I couldn't see to hold fast to those promises if I was always and constantly a bundle of tears because of them.

It was important for me that I not be burdened with grudges or animosity against anyone during this time. I realized those who had said what they had said and done the things that they had done, were only doing what they knew to do. If they felt a person was being rebellious or disobedient, then there was a prescription for that and they felt obligated to fill it. Funny thing, with all my soon-to-encounter trials and situations, I would learn the invaluable lessons that would allow me to be freed from the grudges and animosities expected from one who was not covered by the grace and mercy of their god. And then, to indeed be empowered to stay the course.

So, these hundreds of years after Queen Vashti's dethroning, I found myself "dethroned" as well and my husband (although he had died before realizing his desire) seeking to remarry "one he..." "...found more favor with." What was certain and for sure was that the time I was in right now was genuine and for real – it would take a more "Beautiful Mind" than mine to make up dreams and visions as intricate and complicated as the ones I had been given. Yes, I had seen it all before on God's big screen and had been forewarned. What wasn't exactly clear though was that period of time between when I watched Vashti ride off in her carriage, where I was engulfed and totally overwhelmed with emotions and tears. It was a period of clouded darkness fraught with great rocky obstacles and huge obstructing boulders, pitfalls and potholes. A period where I would have to run relying on my faith and assurance in a God who never fails. That was the place where I was now.

This time now, yes it did symbolize a place of expectancy, peace, contentment, restoration, renewal, and hope. It was also now that I was anticipating the return of everything that had been taken. All I felt that had been stolen was set to be returned: my husband, my home, my emotional and physical health and well-being, my position of respect and esteem with my children, family and my community. As well, all those earthly desires and possessions I felt I wanted to enjoy again were set to return. My God!

The journey to get to here would have taken the imagination of a Shonda Rhimes to come up with. It was all so surreal and many times worse than any nightmare. I had been shown each situation all before they actually happened, and now they were being run on the big screen of my life. Knowing this was a journey chosen for me by God - though many times I prayed for the real-life occurrences to actually be dreams so that I could awaken and free myself from all their consequences.

Unlike the king's Vashti, who, it is assumed, never got to see the one who would replace her, my experience with my Esther would be much different. Not only would I get to see who the young lady was that "pleased the king" – my husband -- over me his 30-year wife, but I would get to participate in many of the same activities and events as she in who he "found favor," in Marshall's eyes and in his heart. My husband was to be commended, though, on how he had remarkably maintained his high standards and taste for beauty and outgoing personality, as was found in this young woman. And that I also had, I am reminded, when he and I first met.

She was petite, with a very pretty face, in her late thirties, and a healthy head full of long, well-maintained hair. Marshall's new "wife-to-be" was an exact duplication of a version of the "me" I had been thirty years before. My "Esther" was without question so much more attractive than the fifty-plus year old mother who was wearing the heaviness and disappointment from years of deferred hope, unrequited love and of not having realized her life's goals and dreams.

Young Esther won hands-down over this woman who was a wife rejected from her youth; and was the overworked, worn ragged, and plum worn out mother of four active children who she had practically raised alone. This was the one Marshall desired instead as his new wife. She was always pleasant, bubbly, and perky – just as I had been... before. Even when I first met her – without knowing the connection she and my husband had, of course – I commented on what an inviting and friendly a personality she had.

I couldn't help speculating on how long she would keep her joyful and "happy-go-lucky" disposition after having lived with the world's most mean-spirited and negative man ever. Or, and to my complete surprise and amazement, would my husband, turn out to be a totally new man with this younger woman, his new bride-to-be. Would he become all that a husband and life mate was expected to be for her – and all of what he had never been to me or for me? Of course, it would have meant that I was the problem and not Marshall, which I could not entertain at the time. There was much too much hurt and pain, disappointment and shame for me to accede to that realization.

Everyone in the room that day when Marshall's anticipated new wife and this hoped-to-be, dethroned wife were introduced, tried to make it seem as though there was nothing going on. It didn't work because the tension in the air was so thick... I could sense something was going on too, between the both of them. Marshall and that young woman were trying desperately to hold on to a secret as they stood trying not to swallow that canary whose feathers were flying around and out from both their mouths. I had now met face to face the source of my pain and agony.

That this was a surreal experience was undeniable because this woman and I could have been twins – thirty years ago. We had similar interests too. We both liked cooking, reading, fashion, singing, home remodeling and decorating. She actually worked at a home and furniture design center; but I charmed family and friends with my ability to interchange our home's décor with little to no monetary investment. So, it was ditto on all those likes for me too. Well, all except working in the Design District. We would both sing on the Praise and Worship Team. She, a soft and melodic Soprano, and I was an uncontrolled, overpowering and forceful Alto.

The church Marshall had begun attending; which the last two children and I all would, eventually - had after-service meals for its members and guests and everyone was encouraged to bring a dish. There arose a competition immediately between us two women to outdo each other with dishes that appealed to his appetite. Marshall was a man who loved deserts and at home had to have one at every meal. So, it was no secret what my contributions would be. My desert specialties were also my husband's favorite, Red Velvet cakes, and Peach Cobblers.

What I had not counted on was that woman learning the only other food for Marshall that could trump a desert. The dishes she came up with were amazingly tasty and appealing. Being from the Keys, it was no secret that my husband's favorite food was any kind of seafood. Marshall's all-time favorites being grouper, shrimp, conch, and lobster. But with two sons in college and another son and daughter in high school, there was no way I could swing for the cost of those.

I had to give it to "My Esther." That young woman outdid herself every week. Some Sundays it was either one of the four seafoods alone, cooked with some amazingly masterful chef-quality smooth and creamy sauce, and plated "just so." Then, on other Sundays, it might be a combination of at least two or all four in another rice pilaf or noodle and sauce dish that was out of this world.

I would always compliment her on the taste and appearance of her dishes until someone spilled the beans. They let it be known that "My Esther" was no genius in the kitchen after all, but that it was another member who was in fact a culinary school graduate who it was that actually cooked every seafood dish that lured away my husband. Now, you know! That was smart, I had to admit. That deception notwithstanding, though, after all the comparisons and similarities, even I had to agree that the always good-natured younger woman was quite a catch for my sixty-four year old husband (though he looked to be in his mid- to late forties), or any other older man who was looking to reconnect with his youth. Unlike his aging wife (now fifty years old) who had too many worries with her kids, with managing her home, paying her bills, and with mounting health woes. My list of "why would he want to be with you now," seemed endless.

However, in spite of all my worries, I looked around at how society viewed women who used their charm and wares to ensnare men. I knew I could do the same to get back all the things I had already lost and those things soon to be stripped away. I would just only need maybe two boyfriends who were very good to me. After all, I wasn't that much for wear and tear compared to other women my age and with just the right amount of fixing up, I could do wonders for helping myself look a whole lot better. Although I had not made myself up in years, I surprisingly, still attracted the attention of men – young and old. Surely, I could use my feminine wiles to get from them all I had lost.

There were many such men who were letting me know that all I had to do was ask. Many still, had hung around after Marshall's passing and through my times of "losing it all" just to ask me, "Is there a-n-y-t-h-i-n-g I can get for you? Is there A-n-y-t-h-i-n-g at all I can do for you?" It was they who put the emphasis on 'anything.' Whether because they felt I was a needy widow; or because they were earnestly attracted to me; for whatever the reason, they hung around.

Except now, circumstances and things were different. Whether they considered me needy or desperate for help and assistance – didn't matter. I had made an agreement with God to follow His path. That meant that I would submit to God's plan and directions so that all Glory and Praise would be to Him -- and not to any man. God would have to let this woman know how I was to walk this new path. What I would have to look out for were the pitfalls, snares, and traps of my past and the interactions and reactions to the events of my present state of affairs and relationships that would try to take me off course.

The one promise of restoration that concerned me most was who could it possibly be that was to become my "new mate." If I was going to go through a life-changing transformation, what was he going to be like? Would he be changing too? How would I really "know" if he was "The One?" The one God had for me would have to be proven, tested and tried himself, as much as I was about to be. Nevertheless, when it was all over and done, God had let me know that ours would be a union on the scale of Scarlet and Rhett Butler or a Ruby Dee and Ossie Davis. Not even Romeo and Juliette would be able to hold a candle to the love we would share. Our divine union would attest to God's ever-abounding grace, mercy, and faithfulness in restoring lives and loves.

Ours would be lives restored by God from the hurts and pains, times of defiance, rebellion and disobedience; and times of questioning our own faith and walk with Him. We would attest to the rewards of being devoted and faithful to living single lives with virtue and dignity, honoring each other's bodies - totally and fully dedicated to serving God. Our union would be looked at by all, Believers and Non-Believers alike, as a testament and attestation to the faithfulness of God's promises for all who committed to overcome their life's tests and trials, who endured and persevered throughout the hardships and challenges. Situations, which for average persons would have meant certain disqualification, destruction, defeat – and many times, death itself.

I knew, too, that I could not make the same mistakes like I had done with my first husband, Marshall. That marriage had been decided purely on all the wrong criteria and had proven disastrous. No, I couldn't, and wouldn't do that again. So, as I prayed to the Father for His guidance and direction, He answered with a list that would cover all of the areas that had caused me to become stuck, resistant and unable to grow into maturity in my relationships. Those situations he knew I would need the most help. The beginning area would be with the lusts of my flesh. This is where I desired most at this point in my life, to feel and experience true physical and intimate satisfaction and gratification. Just the thought sends my body into a whirlwind of sensual longing and expectancy. It was especially in these last thirty years of my life while still a wife to Marshall, that I yearned for and desired a day-in-day-out, 24/7, minute-to minute, all-consuming demonstration of love and affection - - unadulterated intimacy.

MISSION DEFINED

What had quieted my heart during these times of trial and calamity was singing songs of God's faithfulness and love despite man's failings and faults. It wasn't like I was a great singer. Sure, I loved it with a passion, but had always been discouraged by family -- and some choir leaders who felt my voice too powerful and -- loud. When all it really was, is that I was untrained. I had never really learned how to control my voice so I would go from alto to soprano and back again, in the same song – never being quite comfortable with either pitch. But, boy would I give it a go every chance I got.

It was as I was preparing to visit the church just around the corner in my new neighborhood that I heard the song, "Called to Be." I wouldn't refer to that song by that title at first, because what I most remembered was the chorus, "I Will Be What You Call Me to Be." That song's lyrics met me at the very place I was and so it was easy for me to commit it to memory. I didn't catch the name of the singer, but would be too shocked to learn that he was the very same Praise and Worship Leader at the new church I was set to attend in this new neighborhood.

I was certainly grateful for getting to this point, so it did not appear that following this first directive, would create any great difficulty.

> *"Go back to my people. Find a place where your faith will be built up and you can strengthen your spirit in songs of praise and worship of me."*

The church was close enough to be convenient to get to; always had greeters and ushers who were the most pleasant and friendly and I was sure to receive a great message every Sunday. After I had completed the New Member's Orientation class, I inquired about Choir membership. It was so like God to be exact and specific with me during these times, I would be even more grateful for his exactness and specificity when calamity upon calamity and adversity atop adversity would later come upon me. At this faith-building place, I was able to fulfill God's directive to sing "psalms, hymns, and spiritual songs" in worship and honor to him.

The place was known for its strong belief in the principles of Faith. So I would also have the opportunity of fulfilling three other of God's mandates to me at this one place – all the while worshipping in song and singing praises to the one true Lord and Savior. This new place is where I would set my mind and heart to go then. To finally be on my way to what God was calling me to do in order for Him to give back all that had been lost. It was confirmed, this was the place where it would happen. But would it ALL happen here?

What would be encountered here, too, at this place of faith, would be the answer to the first of my greatest desires – restoration of a God-ordained and God-inspired relationship. I would even get to learn through the teachings here what a true God-centered relationship should look like – and what was required of me to be in one. Several relationship opportunities did develop that made the pain of my former love-starved heart overjoyed. Those interested would get to witness me unravel from the "self-assured confident-in-myself" yet God-

113

seeking woman to the confident "God-focused and spirit-driven" Woman of God I was to become. It would be the proving ground for if they could maintain their interest while God's Word transformed and conformed me to his will; proving whether they were actually interested in me – the woman I desperately desired to become. How was I ever to find out, and choose, which one it was that would be the right one for me though?

HER "GREAT CLOUD OF WITNESSES"

They were a great cloud of witnesses and there was one in particular who was looking most intently desperately needing me to master my adversities. That one needed me to somehow come out on top of all I was going through. She was my own daughter. It was two years after the birth of my third son that I was again expecting and resolved that whether this last child born (remembering that I always said I wanted four children) was a girl or not, I would be content. So much else had not been going as I had planned that to set my heart on a girl when that would be the last child, would have been setting myself up for too much disappointment.

My daughter's birth was at a time when I had resolved to abandon the mandate God had given me of being for my husband all that he needed to attain to the stature and measure of the man God desired he become, and to abandon my vow to love him unconditionally. What aided me in dropping my agreement was the problem that my husband wanted nothing to do with such a call from God and had no desire to aspire to or accomplish anything great. So, God released me.

When I was told in the delivery room that the baby was indeed a girl, I could only say, "Thank you, Lord." And what a beautiful baby girl she was, too! Her beauty was a combination of the French, Indian, and Caribbean exotic features from her grandparents and great-grandparents all rolled into one gorgeous bundle of caramel-toned joy. Her skin was a true sundrenched kissable caramel. Her hair was dark, long, and fine-textured in soft curls that went straight whenever it was wet. I had not been much for natural hair growing up and never learned to braid, so it was plaits and ponytails for my little princess. I mixed it up sometimes with either ponytails or plaits and ribbons, or ponytails or plaits with burettes. Those, unfortunately, were the only options I could offer my beautiful baby girl until she grew up and learned how to do amazing things herself with her very versatile hair.

What it was is that this young woman, my fourth child and only daughter, now had a family of her own and had been emulating and fashioning many of her life's choices by what she saw and heard from this woman she knew growing up. That woman was once the epitome of a successful female in that daughter's eyes. She would watch me struggle to finish my education all the while empowering my children to be independent, industrious, and hardworking. And then to see them all go on to attend college themselves.

That daughter saw me maintain my dignity and self-respect with an abusive and difficult husband. She witnessed as I interacted with professionals and educators, and though while not always starting out calm and in control, always managing to reach a level of poised professionalism. She saw her mother as a life-long learner.

My daughter had been born just at that time when I had said to myself, "Enough! I will no longer sacrifice or forfeit my life's goals and dreams for the sake of getting along with someone who did not desire the very best for my life. That someone was my husband, Marshall. This daughter had seen me manage our home, seemingly single-handedly care for her and her three brothers, start and graduate college after twenty years of being out of high school; and, so that I could be on a schedule with my younger set of children, obtain a full-time position at their local elementary school. Getting to ride to and from school with their mother was a big deal for my kids. I could see it brought such a thrill and sense of security to this daughter and son to have their mother so active and involved in their lives.

It would be at the time they were entering middle school that I would become ill. Never would I fully realize the devastation my children would experience seeing such a complete turnaround in a life that had seemed unstoppable. It was crucial that I recover -- especially for this daughter. She idolized and admired me most of all my children and, as a mother herself now, it was she who would be the next generation to demonstrate what her family's lifestyle would be like. After all, my daughter had made up in her mind that she would copy the pathway to success this mother was travelling – until that mother became ill.

My illness would last three years. In those years, there were more times that I would spend in the Emergency Rooms of our local hospitals than at home. Then, when I was at home, my time would be spent caring for my own basic needs and feeding on the Word of God. I would get up early in the morning, make coffee, and put on breakfast for myself and my kids. On my way back to my bedroom, I would stop by the bathroom to brush up and clean up. I had given the job of getting our son and daughter off to school to Marshall and I would only check up every now and then to make sure they were on task and not leaving late. My children appeared to be managing quite well for themselves. Next thing I would do was to spend time in the Word and watching TBN. Before I realized it, three years had passed.

Recovery happened for me one day when I decided I had experienced enough doctor and emergency room visits. I determined there was never going to be a fabricated pill that would heal me of whatever emotional or physical ailment I had. I resolved that if the Word of God were true, then I would much rather go that route – with trusting God to heal me of all my ailments. What I did was to stop taking the psychotropic medications, cancelled all doctor visits, and prayed that God would take control of everything concerning my health and mental well-being. I would test the validity of my healing and ability to get on with life by getting a job. I knew that God was answering my prayers -- and that he had a sense of humor -- when I landed the position at a local Mental Health facility.

After recovering, I got back on my path of supporting myself and my kids, and back to finally planning to make the break with Marshall. It was not to happen that way because now was when we discovered the existence and severity of his medical condition. It was in "the fall of November" (how ironic) and I would be nurse and caregiver to him for nearly three years. Marshall would succumb to his terminal condition just one week shy of our thirtieth wedding anniversary.

In our earlier years of married life Marshall and I had worked together to be sure we had a nest egg when we both retired. Unfortunately, what was supposed to be more than enough funds stashed away, after Marshall's passing were now being rapidly depleted. I was helping others and attempting to maintain the home without the benefit of additional income from employment. Was this mother who had always preached to her children extolling the virtues of financial and social responsibility based upon living by Godly principles, to now endure the consequences of irresponsible financial decisions and suffer insurmountable losses. Even more important, would she, and could she recover from those losses. Would I overcome and prevail, or fail miserably.

The beautiful and gifted young woman, my only daughter, whose name meant "Intelligent Jewel," because of the unique bond we shared, had her very deepest emotions and life expectations tied into the success or failure of her mother's actions. Yes, she had heard of all my stories of the harshness and hardships of both her father's childhood and my life as a child. My daughter had witnessed this mother navigate through the unknowns and complexities of assuring my children had the very best educational opportunities their school district had to offer. She knew her mother to go to bat for those children whenever they encountered inequities from school administrators or teachers.

My daughter had witnessed the transformation of her mother from a passive and blindly submissive wife to one who was assertive and outspoken – who took charge of her life and did not allow one who wasn't leading at all to control her. A woman who had determined that enough was enough of a life lived as part of a team - yet never experiencing the bond that was to connect them. It had to be the loneliest of existences.

This daughter had also been the silent observer throughout all the situations her mother had experienced involving her father and my Esther. She had even unknowingly

119

accompanied her Dad to places where that younger woman would be and watched silently as they acted out their "new lover's" cat and mouse game. My only daughter had sat with her Dad and witnessed as I sang alongside that young woman in the choir noticing all along her Dad's eyes fixed and gazing only at the younger woman.

My child had watched as I desperately attempted to maintain my dignity and pride throughout all the losses. Those losses that would include our home, the last of our finances; and having to move into a condominium owned by family. Although I was able to renovate, update, and transform that condominium into one which was much more comfortable and had many family members commenting that it resembled our old home.

Then, my precious child would observe as I slowly took steps to renew my involvement and participation in community and neighborhood activities, and to begin attending family get-to-gethers and social events. This daughter had accompanied me on my many appointments to doctor and lawyer offices and was by my side during times when my escapades took me to court and local government offices as well. The times when she needed to be my mouthpiece, I was pleasantly surprised to witness her poise and professionalism. She handled herself quite well.

As the youngest of my four children, my daughter had maintained a respect and admiration for me throughout all those difficult times. Now, after I had exhausted all means of reserve finances, was also at a place where my income was not sufficient to meet my monthly expenses, and was facing a major decision of how I would replace them, my child was waiting to see what choices her mother would make. I had taught her independence and to lean on her own abilities, skills, training and expertise in working through the issues and challenges of her young life, always looking to God for direction. Now, when I would have to call upon those same principles and wisdom from that same guidance and direction I had poured into her and her brothers, it was she, my only girl child, who would be the principal witness to how her mother would maneuver through her challenges.

Realizing the magnitude of this situation with my daughter brought even greater focus and clarity to my mission. I had to succeed! God give me strength! Sure, there were any number of flesh-driven, ways of the world schemes, I could have devised. It was even in agreeing to become engaged to my fiancé that I felt at least I was following the acceptable traditions of society. Surely that would put me in good stead with my child. I was not choosing to be a promiscuous woman by having all types of different men coming and going out of my place. Surely she saw that relationship as an honorable one. But, sad to say, I don't really think that she did. Neither did her demeanor nor her facial expressions ever say, "I'm proud of you Mom." All the more reason to have answered God's question of "Where are you" with, "Not where you called me to be, Lord." My daughter knew that too.

So, it was neither in becoming engaged, nor in following what would have been the more expedient and popular means of increasing my income – more popularly and truthfully stated as, having a "sugar daddy" to take care of me, that I was to resort to. It was God's Word that had to be my only source of direction. From my reading in the Book of Psalms, the route to my recovery first became crystal clear to me. Many of that book's collection of lyrical poems, were written for various reasons including for those of appreciation, gratitude and thanksgiving or simply to extoll the virtue of singing praises to the Lord God. To finally be at a place where I could say, "I surrender all" and "I will do what you call me to do" brought much peace to me.

So, to accomplish what I had been called to do first by God was obvious. I had to re-commit and re-submit. God was calling me to re-submit to spiritual leadership and re-commit to spiritual authority. I was to humble myself under the authority of Godly leadership. It would be by faith and in a spirit of worship and praise that I was to return.

CHAPTER FOUR

CONFIRMATION

*"A single witness shall not rise up against a man on account
of any iniquity or any sin which he has committed; on the
evidence of two or three witnesses a matter shall be
confirmed. Deut. 19:15*

*And they went out and preached everywhere, while the
Lord worked with them, and confirmed the word by the
signs that followed...*
Mark 16:20

*When it feels like everything is falling apart
God is usually putting it all back together.*
Unknown

DECISIONS & CHOICES, DEFINING LIFE EVENTS

The intentions of those interested in dating me had been made perfectly clear. The time had come that I must decide and make a choice of who it would be I would "give myself and my heart to." Who it was I would join in working to fulfill God's mandate for his kingdom. All other factors of my restoration would be based on this choice. This was big! It should have been well known that whoever it would be, because of my love-starved condition, all my desires would be towards him. I would be totally and completely, his – wholly and altogether. There would be no turning back for me. Thing was though, I couldn't allow myself to make that decision – not while fighting so hard against the overpowering feelings, desires, longings and need for intimacy I was experiencing.

I was a real mess. One touch could have set me off on an X-rated fantasy of emotional and physical fulfillment to match the raciest of porn videos. Christian Grey's Anastasia Steele's recount of her first experience of the joy of reaching her climactic explosion had nothing on what my inner sexual deviate contrived. So, I stayed to myself and didn't allow myself to be touched by any of them. A couple did get in a sneak kiss on the cheek and short hug; but I couldn't allow much more. How could I make an intelligent choice of "the right one" while fighting against the onslaught of such raging physical desires and emotions. They had to be quieted and "shut down" before I could proceed. So, if I weren't to go with the one who most excited me physically, then on what would I rely my decision? And on what would I base it?

True, I was a bit of an enigma to most people. Although super-friendly and helpful, I kept mostly to myself, not venturing into close relationships with either men, or other women. I had learned much from my brief contacts and interactions with those who showed interest in me though. Things like what it was that attracted me most; and what it was that repulsed me completely. I had found that a quality those who most attracted me possessed was the simple bravery of talking to me -- actually holding meaningful conversations - even though I most often responded in shock and tongue-tied silence.

To have these fine men actually addressing me was more than this heart could bear so I hardly ever responded with anything of substance. Still, they were the ones who touched my heart most. Such occasions were not many, but whenever they did happen, boy oh boy, did I cherish and relish their every word.

Another thing I knew for sure was that I would not do the same thing I had done with Marshall. That one was an accident waiting to happen, having been decided purely on all the wrong, yet socially accepted and culturally popular, criteria. Standards of the times, which were employed by almost everyone, yes, but destined for failure and divorce – as was evidenced in our culture's soaring divorce rate. Adhering to that set of values - looks, money (or potential to get wealth), and position (power or fame), - had proven disastrous. I couldn't and wouldn't do it again. No, I couldn't repeat that same foolishness.

So, as I prayed to the Father for His guidance and direction, God answered with a list that would cover all of the areas He knew I would need healing and release from to get to the place He, most importantly, and I, so desperately, desired. Those areas turned out to be places of major life-defining situations for me that held the most trauma, emotional tragedy, and heartbreak. I would live with the impression of them throughout the different seasons and phases of my life never quite mastering their lessons and always doing a repeat. God knew I needed closure first in order to go forward in victory to the fulfillment of the Divine Plan he had for me.

THE TWO SISTERS DOWN THE WALKWAY

The first life-defining event to influence my relationship decisions happened when as a child growing up in our family of five girls. Mama was a single parent and there was no man in the house. Well, there was no man except those who came to visit Mama; but who in the wee hours of the mornings, sometimes made their way to our bedroom. It was when we all lived in a two-bedroom apartment at one end of a one-story, three-unit green apartment building, appropriately called "The Green Side." I later learned that this little two-block community would become notorious for gangs and violence. My younger sister, my twin, and I, along with my two older sisters, would be the victims of many of those acts of violence. What I recall about that place was that there were two sisters, who occupied each of the other two units in our building.

Those sisters were always immaculately dressed and coiffed, nothing like any of the other women my sisters or I had ever seen. That wasn't really saying much, since we didn't get to venture very far from our apartment units. What I do recall most is that those sisters were not very friendly at all. Even as small six or seven year olds, my sister and I would approach the women asking some silly little-girl questions only to always be put off and dismissed.

The most difficult times to accept were when we girls were in danger and being abused. It didn't seem to matter to those two at all. Even though most other people were eager to give special attention to my sister and me, because we were twins, not so with these two women. Their self-absorption was so strong; they could care less that we twins were mannerly,

127

respectful, and studious. I felt my sister and I at least deserved encouragement to do well and to keep trying hard -- to be encouraged to continue on to the path of success. But, what we got instead was – nothing. Maybe that was a good thing. God was keeping us from falling into the same pit those two sisters had dug for themselves that had them doing whatever it was to maintain lifestyles that afforded them the prestige and comfort they were obviously enjoying.

What those two women did have in common that caused the pain for me, as I would begin my time of testing was that they had constant overnight visitors. Different men would arrive in the early hours of the evening as darkness was approaching, and leave just before sunrise. We girls knew this because we would keep up with who visited which sister and when it was they came and left. It was because those two closed their eyes to all that was going on with us in our times of desperate need; to say nothing of never showing any signs of friendliness that intrigued us so about them. I would resolve in my heart what I would take away from these women's influence.

Yes, I would strive to dress well and speak well, but I vowed to always consider young children and befriend them as often as I could. I would never fail to offer some gesture or word of encouragement. Also, and most importantly, I would never, have different men coming in and out of my home like those women did – no matter the reason. Even at my young age, although I didn't know the specifics of what was going on, I did know that something was wrong with what they were doing.

THE PLIGHT OF NEEDY WOMEN

The next situation from my past that I would have to overcome happened for me when as a young woman in a career position working in downtown Miami. Even then, I loved to cook and would share many of my meals with neighbors. It was one evening, after sharing with several of those neighbors that, in my naïveté, I realized this one male neighbor had stayed after all the others were gone. He immediately made it known that he wanted to be intimate with me but I wanted nothing to do with that – or him. Sure, he knew I lived alone and had no male visitors and told me as much. His point was that since I was a young attractive woman, I had to have a need for sex and he was here to fill that need. He was right; I wasn't in a relationship with anyone and would have welcomed his advance under circumstances of dire desperation. However, the fact was that I was not attracted to him and was too in control of my body's needs to indulge myself with just anyone.

That neighbor realized that I was not buying the idea of satisfying myself for the sake of satisfying myself and began to proposition me – a very wrong move. He offered to buy me all sorts of nice things and to give me whatever amount of money I desired. Well, I either had my own of all he was offering me, or could buy it myself. The whole idea of his mindset to seduce me greatly repulsed me. So, while showing him the door, he remarked, "I know what you need. You need about three or four children. You'll be glad to have somebody like me to help you out then."

That comment stuck with me and created such a great fear for having children without the safety and security of being in a loving marriage with a husband who shared in the parenting of our children. I couldn't repeat the family lifestyle that my mother had created. We were eventually seven children fathered by five different men. My mother had been looking for love and had given away what she thought would secure that love. Then, when we children came, she was forced to do whatever it took to keep us clothed and fed. I could not allow that to happen to me.   Whenever I did have children, my "Pollyanna," "Live happily ever after" "fairytale" mindset, told me that my husband and I would be well able and willing to take care of them – together. To have sole responsibility scared me senseless. I had to be careful to never allow myself to be put in a position of "need" or "want" that would cause me to depend on someone the likes of that fellow.

So, when married to Marshall and he decides that I should leave (abandoning our children to someone who had never shared in the responsibility of parenting them), providing no means of support for either them or myself, I was sent into a psychological whirlwind. Feelings of the greatest fear and dread overtook me.

Of course, thirty years after that interaction with my horny neighbor, I could still connect Marshall's demand with those feeling from my earlier years. Sure, I had those four children at this time but two had made it off to college. The two still left at home were really catching it. Yes, I had the husband like I had assured myself of years ago that I felt confident would keep me from being in a situation where I would not have help in raising and supporting my children. How wrong I was. That fact was emphasized and brought home in the worst way and at the worst possible time.

While I was recovering from my three-year period of illness, my youngest and third-born son and only daughter and last-born child, were left to their own devices. Their father never took charge of parenting them or seeing to their needs. Therefore, in my time of recuperation, I began to pray to God that he would cover and shield them. God answered with a promise that he would indeed see my children through their trials and adversities, and that "'all would be well' for all my children; especially the last two."

NOT THAT WOMAN'S HUSBAND

It was my next life experience where I would have to overcome decisions I had made following the ignorant and arrogant mindset of society's permissiveness and my youthful depravity. I was actually almost twenty-eight years old when, starving for love, attention and affection, that time I decided to leave Marshall. Those six years of marriage had been living hell on earth. I had been working with an attorney's office for a year and saved up enough money to feel that I could support the three of us when I returned to Miami. What I did was to unite with someone who had shown and proven an undying interest in me from years before. I had done a great job of maintaining my distance from this man who held a very high and prestigious local government position. Fleeing from such a love-deprived place with my husband and returning to a place where my femininity and desirability was affirmed and admired, I cast off all cares and allowed myself to flirt with that married man. It was actually much more than flirting. We had a torrid love affair with insatiable desires on both our parts. He wanted me as much as I needed him – but because of his health issues and my unwillingness to fully and completely devote myself to him - denying my boys the time they needed with me - neither of us achieved the fulfillment we so desperately desired. Still, there were no limits to the times he and I put our all into trying to thoroughly enjoy each other's companionship.

Our times of communication were when I realized how very much I enjoyed sharing my heart and mind - in the simple act of just talking. Try as I might, I hadn't been successful in doing that with Marshall. So I was starved for much more than just physical affection. I couldn't ever recall being so emotionally fulfilled – being the recipient of this man's wisdom and insight through our many discussions. Although I was twenty years his junior and pretty much self-taught, not yet having obtained my college degree, I found we had mutually insightful and engaging conversations. He was as intrigued with my contributions as I was blown away by his.

Our talks were always soul satisfying and quenched all my cravings for intellectual stimulation, social interaction and engagement. We would enjoy midnight cruises aboard private yachts and flights to Broadway shows with carriage rides through Central Park and eating dinner at five-star restaurants sitting just feet from live jazz bands. I saw him as a "super intellect." He was well read and so very knowledgeable of local, state, national, and international happenings. I was truly enamored of him. It was during this relationship that I would be introduced to many of the community and religious leaders in our tri-county area. They were the lawyers and judges, school principals, teachers and professionals, including local, state, and federal government officials and dignitaries. The list of ministers, preachers, and church officials I was introduced to at that time surely remembered me from those back then. Many of them I was still interacting with these thirty years later.

Also, remembering me would be the sorority sisters of the wife of that married man I was carrying on with. I was sure those sorority sisters, community and religious leaders, and the sons of that married man all would recall his and my disrespectful antics. That both he, then his wife, had passed many years ago did not erase the impact of what was a very public, private love affair. No, their deaths did not resolve or remove what I had done – and his sons would remember well. I still recall running into one of those sons and desperately desiring to ask him to forgive me. Unfortunately, I wasn't at the place of total brokenness and repentance at that time – not like I was now. Yes, I had learned to forgive myself, but many of them still showed that they were nowhere near the place of forgiving me - letting me know in no uncertain terms every chance they got. It would be God's assurance of His forgiveness that allowed me to walk among them in the truth of who I now was.

So, for me, it would be these three life-defining situations that God would use to test me to see how I would respond to the unmet needs in my life. He would allow those early influences that had shaped me into the guarded and untrusting person I was today. Had His Word made the change He desired in my heart? The opportunity to challenge my faith came when I had lost it all -- and was in dire and desperate need of help. There were decisions I had to make that would answer those challenges.

HER KINSMEN REDEEMERS, MEN SHE'D MEET -
"FOR REAL" GHETTO GANGSTAS & THUGS

Of those waiting for my decision, and who felt that I was a real "ghetto chick" was one I'd encounter at a time when I had not walked according to God's perfect design since the passing of my husband. Once, when feeling like I was at a Sara and Abraham phase of my walk; fearing having the issues of my life exposed for all to see, and that I might never see the fulfillment of God's promises, I allowed myself to become "engaged." Yeah, and yes he did, "put a ring on it." And simply because of the sheer forcefulness of that man, I can only describe it as I "allowed" myself to accept. Even though I did ask for some time to consider his proposal, secretly I feared that he was as good as it was going to get for someone like me. So, sooner than I ever should have or wanted to, I told him, "Yes, I'll marry you." So, I became engaged for the second time in my life. And although the feeling wasn't as overwhelming as with Marshall, I still felt awful. So much wasn't right.

He was nothing at all like the professional type man I was attracted to - well educated and literate. Even his physical attributes went against the grain of what I was accustomed to. But something he did have that other men could have copied was that he showed a deep and burning desire for me and promised that he would work his hardest to satisfy my every need and longing. And, he did – work his hardest. Although he was someone I could engage in open, passionate, and lively discussions and conversations, they were not the deep cerebrally and intellectually stimulating kind I craved. There was this gut feeling too that I did not know his whole story. Somehow, I felt he had a deep secret that had much to do with his feeling more comfortable living in confined and cramped surroundings. He showed many of the same signs that my ex-con family members did when they were released after so many years of incarceration. They could be quite content and comfortable living in a corner of the smallest of teeny tiny places they called home. So strange. However, I never asked and he never did volunteer the information.

In spite of that, I felt like the treasure this man had been searching for all his life. Every time we were in the presence of others, he made sure I felt like I was the only reason he woke up that day. Moreover, he could tell me more about myself than I ever realized I was letting on to. And it was all true. He said he had been studying me since the very first day we met, using the principle from 1 Peter 3:7, to find out about me.

Husbands, likewise, dwell with them with understanding, giving honor to the wife, as to the weaker vessel, and as being heirs together of the grace of life, that your prayers may not be hindered. (NKJ)

Likewise, ye husbands, dwell with them according to knowledge, giving honour unto the wife, as unto the weaker vessel, and as being heirs together of the grace of life; that your prayers be not hindered. (KJV)

A brief study of a Christian Relationship writer's interpretation of this scripture shows us his view, as the usual interpretation, which I have heard in many sermons and talks, is that a husband should seek to understand his wife, with the goal of making decisions sensitive to her needs. Indeed, I was in full and complete agreement that a man should work at knowing his wife better. He should probe for the roots of her ways of thinking. He should try to discover her innermost fears, hopes, and desires. Above all, as many experts on family living recommend, he should let his wife talk to him. I could only imagine what an amazing relationship Marshall and I would have had if he had done any one of those should'ves.

Talking with my fiancé was like talking to a life-long, intimate friend. I would try my very best to overlook his shortcomings and make the best of our impending marriage. Yes, I would try... But God. It was my Father who had let me know, once again by asking me that "Adam in the Garden trying to hide behind a fig leaf question," "Where are you?" That familiar voice again, exactly like the one I had heard when I was running down that dark and rocky road. It was as clear as if someone were standing right beside me in the confines of that small hole-in-the-wall, "honey comb" of a room where I had been hidden and stowed away like a priceless treasure. It was as though I had been placed there in the hopes that he could keep me away from the others. They were many who had let him know that they wanted me, too. A band of desperately looking, hard-working blue-color men who felt they could revive their sex lives with the likes of a woman like me.

Although my fiancé tried his all to be for me everything I desired and more, I knew - and maybe he too realized – that he could never be. What we were trying to put together would not ever, and could not ever, work. I was not only out of place, but once again in a relationship where I was out of God's

Perfect Will. And that fact was far more critical to me. That I would be fulfilling God's Divine & Perfect Will, Purpose and Plan in this phase of my journey to restoration. I prayed, "Forgive me for growing weary, giving up, and 'settling'."

It was the only truthful response I could give. So I left there, our hole-in-the-wall honeycomb – leaving him, my fiancé – never, ever to return. It would take a while for me to be delivered from his early morning calls of, "How are you, I was just thinking about you. Do you need anything? I can come right over and get whatever it is for you?" Those calls never failed to ignite the old emotions I was asking God to cleanse me of. I would repent, recommit, and realign myself to return to God's plan of how I was to walk out my issues - given through His Divine Word.

Many men, and women, would reveal their intentions towards me. I was not quite sure how it was that women had seen me as a possible mate and companion, but they were many – and they were quite wrong. Yes, I was friendly with everyone I met. And, no, I had no prejudices against them. But, that I wanted to have an intimate relationship with any one of them was absurd. Still, those men who let me know they desired the me they saw on the outside -- not having a clue to those issues that were eating away just underneath the surface on the inside of me -- were a handsome, very worthy and desirable bunch. Problem was my deliverance and healing required I submit all my life's hurts, pains, disappointments and desires to God's special blue print and roadmap – and not to them.

The difficulty my position posed for me was that I could not be anything but absolutely certain it was God saying, "Yes. He is the One. That one is to be your redeemer." What I had to do, then, was to make sure I kept up my guard and focused on His Word. GUARD AND FOCUS, GIRL! GUARD AND FOCUS!

THE VOICE

It was music, worshipping and singing songs of praise that had sustained me through all of my painful and trying times of discovering how it was I would maintain my position as Marshall's wife. Being "the other woman" to my husband's "more preferred one" took its toll on my self-esteem though. It would be God's promises put to song that always brought back comfort and focus to the challenges I faced. Songs affirming that I was special, "The One" and affirming that I was "The Only Answer to Their Heart's Cry And Desire." I was fully affirmed of the Love God had for me in melodies and tunes that soothed my aching heart. So, it was those singing songs, playing their instruments, or who were skilled enough to do both, who drew my interest in those times.

The first man of music to approach me, had a voice that was deep and gravelly, and it made quite an impression on me too. He was a "Psalter" and it was his singing style that captured my attention. The songs were excessively antiquated and irrelevant to the times, but his low, raspy, husky and "smoky room" sound caused me to...fantasize that just maybe... we could... he and I.... possibly, maybe consider. He was the one who had made the very real and first advance towards me since Marshall's death and once I'd finally decided to allow myself the freedom of mingling with others again. I didn't realize it as that, at first; him making an advance towards me. But, his intentions were confirmed that time he saw me, and taking my hand, planted a big kiss on it – not once, but three times. Not only did I notice, but everyone around us knew something was up as well.

It felt perfectly fine and okay for me, a four-year widow, to sit and fantasize about the skillful singer of songs. But, an open exhibition of affection by laying on my hand that many kisses went way beyond any semblance of a friendly brotherly "good to see you" greeting. I could hear all who were standing around us let out the loudest gasp. His actions so shocked me that I believe I heard one from myself as well.

I would learn that the gifted crooner was very married with a wife who was experiencing multiple medical challenges and health complications. Hmmm, a sick spouse and a wandering caregiver. This would have been a set-up for the very same type situation I had experienced with my own husband happening all over again – except I would have been the Esther to this man's poor ailing wife. This was a perfect setup for the enemy to my destiny to say, "See, she gave in to her lustful desires. There was no God-purpose in her." Upon learning of my crooner's intentions by this very open and blatant display, it was so clear to me that I had to leave out of there with a quickness. And I did!

"WANNA BE" GANGSTAS, THUGS, & SEXUAL DEVIATES

What repulsed me most of those who showed any interest in me at all, were the ones who somehow felt that I was attracted to treatment and interaction by Ghetto-style, 'Gangsta-types," with "street swag," and "hood" credibility. How could they not know how very far from reality their assessments were? They would stand swaying to one side with their hands folded on their chests and giving a "What's up," nod in my direction. They would then break out into a jailhouse pose while leaning their bodies and heads to the side, imitating "Hood" swag. I should have checked myself. Did I really look like a "Ghetto Hood Chick?" It troubled me greatly that their assessment created such an impression. Nevertheless, their comical and animated actions somehow were actually an attraction for me to them. At least it showed they had a sense of humor – even though it felt at my expense. I sometimes considered entertaining their advances, if not for just the mere fact of getting to ask them, "What were you thinking?"

Although those gangstas and thugs were the types I grew up with and around, I had spent my whole life running away from them. They were way too street smart for me since all my smarts were from books and the little I learned from my sisters and mother.

The "sexual deviates" were the ones who sat and made overt sexual innuendoes by working their knees together, simulating visible self-masturbation, and sexual arousal. Their eyes would be fixed on me but there was no way I would give them the pleasure of returning the gaze. I was too disgusted. And still, the one who, while pointing to me, would gesture to a friend how he would throw my legs over his shoulder and "go in." That one I would have to forgive for so many vulgarities and instances of "depraved indifference."

What did attract me most were the ones who had enough confidence to be themselves upon approaching me without any preconceived notions or ideations of where I'd come from, or where and what season I was presently in, at this point in my life. The ones who, in their confident assurance, looked at me with eyes of understanding and unconditional acceptance. They were the ones whose touch made me feel most secure and protected. The ones, too, who were brave enough to actually approach me with their sincere, meaningful, and heartfelt touches. The ones who got close enough to me that I could "see them" through their eyes.

Their "touches" were most times with their eye contact alone, but they were still felt in my heart. I had been shocked to receive from a couple of them a cheek kiss - ever so innocently – but, it was still a kiss - that told me so much about them. The one who gave me the biggest and tightest hug ever was the same one whose paths and visions were intertwined with mine. I didn't quite know what to make of that one, or of his gesture. I so wanted to return the sentiment of his hug, but there was so much going on that interfered with my feeling the freedom to do so. So, I "left him hanging" as they say.

He recognized my reluctance and responded with a puzzled look. I simply smiled and gave a sheepish grin. This was a strained and strange relationship to say the least. He was one of those who she felt didn't have a clue as to who she really was or what she was really all about. Except for that one attempt of his, he was pretty much like the others who caused her to feel like some diseased, unapproachable, untouchable alien.

It seemed God truly had his work cut out for him from this bunch of fine fellows. If the work he was doing in my life was anything like he would need to do in theirs, he truly was a miracle working God. There was not a one I could finger as my "him," "my Redeemer" at this point. I would wait on God to do what only he could do in their lives -- and in mine.

CONTROLLING VASHTI'S LUSTS OF HER EYES, HER FLESH, AND HER PRIDE OF LIFE

So, I wouldn't be a woman who had men coming in and out of my house at all times of the day and night. And I wouldn't allow myself to be considered deserving of treatment in a thuggish, ghetto or hood manner. And neither would I betray the sanctity of another woman's marriage by engaging in a relationship with her husband; or, God forbid, having him to leave her for me. And, since I loathed the idea of doing "whatever it takes" to get money and things from men, I would not, and could not become anyone's "side piece." I had experienced what it felt like to be loved by someone, although not God's perfected best for me, who made me feel loved in ways I had only dreamed of. Problem was, it seemed I was closing the door on what appeared to be my only options.

If I were considering the qualities popular with Bible-toting, Spirit-filled, Tongue-talking Christians as the ones to be used in choosing my mate and couldn't, what on earth was I supposed to do. So then, the question I considered instead became whether I should consider their looks, or their physiques, their finances and wealth, their ability to express their God-given gifts, or their notoriety and fame? They each stood out in one or more of those characteristics. But no one suitor had them all. Just what was I to use in making my decision? If, then, they were all considered to be faithful, committed, Spirit-filled, Spirit-led and Tongue-Talking Men of God, was the more appropriate question, "What was it I was filled with, guided and influenced by?" The answer to that would allow me to accomplish the task at hand.

145

WALLS AND MASKS

We tend to look at the lives of those considered normal and believe that they are automatically equipped with the tools that help them to successfully navigate through their circumstances of life. Not so. But even though I had head knowledge of that fact, I still felt that the things missing since my early childhood developmental years caused me to be dysfunctional in this area of feeling "normal." Important nurturing tools had not been taught or instilled in me to provide for psychological and emotional confidence, assurance, and strength. They would have been what I would need to be equipped for such a life-altering decision as I was facing.

Although many interpreted my persona at this season of my life to be one of a self-assured, self-confident, and secure person -- the opposite was more the truth. I had never quite developed a wholesome, emotionally mature self-worth and personal value. My personality was fraught with self-doubt, low self-esteem, inadequacy, and unworthiness. What I had done was to construct walls and create masks for myself. I hid behind those so that the real "me" -- that fragile woman who just didn't feel she measured up -- would be hidden and protected.

So, as I pondered the work to be done on unmasking me, I also entertained another set of qualities in a mate that I was on guard to watch out for. Those were the ones I had used those many years ago when considering marriage to Marshall. They were the superficial symbols of status and worth, the world-idolizing values of physical looks and attractiveness, the money, the education, the car, and the clothes – the true lusts of the eyes and pride of life.

Yes, I had fallen for all of those false attributes of a person's worth, and came to realize very shortly after marriage that, although financial well-being and security were unquestionably very important; more important to be desired was a God-inspired, mutually loving and respectful relationship that such superficial attributes could never insure. So, though it had taken thirty long years of waiting for my mate to align with God's plan for us both -- when that didn't happen, I realized I had been given the unique opportunity by God to learn to discern those qualities on my own. There had been a divine set-up that allowed me to recognize what a spiritually and emotionally rewarding relationship truly was. That type intimacy was so what I longed for and sought to experience – if only I could hold on until it manifested.

TOOLS TO GOD'S RESTORATION -
MANTRAS, SCRIPTURES, LIFE EXAMPLES

A whole lot of help is what I would need to avoid the areas where I had fallen before. During the time of my three-year recuperation from physical, emotional, and psychological attacks, God first gave me a "Mantra, "I will not forfeit the Divine Purpose and Plan God has for my life for the temporal, soulish, flesh-driven, and lust-filled desires, pleasures, fornications and whoredoms of this world."

Those words came together in my Spirit as I studied scriptures on lust and God's purposes and plans for our lives. I had to know what God's Word said about those desires so that I would be assured of the Father's covering. The place I was at was where my desires to fulfill the overwhelming physical urges for intimacy could so willingly and easily be satiated by any one of those potential and oh-so-eager-to-please redeemers. Fortitude was needed that was way beyond what I was physically able to manifest. There had to be the greatest consequence for me giving in, too. If all the promises God had made were "forfeited" because of a sensual and sexual indulgence, how sad would that be. My family stood to have everything restored to us. I could not be the reason that all would be lost and sacrificed at the altar of fornication and whorish lust-filled indulgences.

No, I couldn't and I wouldn't. Even though some of those brothers were drop-dead, gorgeous and beastly physically fit with all the right equipment to get the job done of fulfilling my desires in right fashion. See, "Whoa, girl!" Pull up and check yourself. That's how easily it happened. Just the thought got me to going in...

Since all those showing an interest had one or more outstanding physical feature that was appealing to me, I couldn't use such a superficial criteria as that either. Some had just the right height with the dark and handsome added in. And there was one tan man in a tan suit that just to look at him astounded me and took me to a place...

Still others were just the right height, build, or had looks to attract the most discerning of women. So great was my desire at this time that I could reach that place every woman dreamed of getting to during intimate engagements just looking at many of those men – and imagining... Even the ones, who weren't in either of the categories of great bodies or super good looks, still had sensually engaging manly sex appeals that were oh so very hard to fight off.

It did my condition absolutely no good whatsoever to allow my mind to daydream, fantasize, or hallucinate about engaging in physical intimacy. Since I had experienced the lack of that very thing my life long, I had made myself believe that there was something "wrong" with me. Truth be told, I felt that way 'all' of my adult life including the thirty years of my marriage. What I had uncovered about myself was that, contrary to popular belief, I did possess a very strong desire for intimacy and sexual fulfillment that had yet to be satisfied. Sure, I suppressed it because in the marriage relationship I had been in, there was only either disappointment or rejection.

Disappointment in the failure to engage in and reach satisfaction; and rejection by the only one who it was expected a wife was to receive intimate and sexual enjoyment and fulfillment. Yet and still, I could not allow that unfulfilled need and desire to cause me to forfeit all. I was determined to GUARD AND FOCUS! Repeating the Mantra as many times as it took continuing to always, GUARD AND FOCUS! I will not forfeit the Divine Purpose and Plan God has for my life for the temporal, soulish, flesh-driven, and lust-filled desires, pleasures, fornications, and whoredoms of this world."

Of my redeemer candidates' talents - some being musicians, singers, educators, and still others street-smart entrepreneurs, all were impressive and accomplished in their own rights. Although I gravitated more towards musicians and singers, I couldn't bear the thought of not having my intellect stimulated as well. Having spent over thirty years with someone who barely spoke to me and whose only passionate conversations were sparse to none at best. What was offered as communication were either questions about what would be prepared for the upcoming Sunday or holiday dinner – or, how well or badly his favorite sports team had played. I could not and would not endure that again.

Sure, I was in the process of discovering my real confident and self-assured self as well, but to settle again in life with an emotional cripple incapable of engaging in meaningful and effective communication or life activities and opportunities, was not an option. There were some of those men who were world-famous entertainers and as exciting as that may have sounded to some women, I did not relish the idea of riding on the coattails of someone else's fame and fortune. They had to be willing to help me to achieve those dreams, hopes, and visions I had - however humble. Their fame was their fame.

Then, the offers of those who used their wealth to entice me with cars, homes, and money were so very appealing. Those usually came with a great degree of me having to accept a hidden insufficiency or inadequacy at some level. Those deficiencies would be exhibited predominantly by an inability to perform intimate acts. Whether the dysfunctions were brought on due to advancing age; having overindulged and been over-zealous in fulfilling their youthful pleasures; or whether they were fulfilling some "throw the virgin in the bed with the king to revive him" fantasy due to advancing illness and the desire to partake in life's last pleasures before their end.

The problem for me with this was obvious. The opportunity I would be denied to enjoy what I had lacked for so many years was not promised. I was not willing to settle for a fully furnished four walls and a roof, or a shiny new car with DeLorean doors, convertible roofs, 22-inch or 24-inch rims, or... Whew! Boy, those things did sound so enticing! But for what object could I swap God's promises? Neither was there any amount of money that they offered that could, or would ever, compensate for my loss. To never, ever experience the passion and pleasure of true intimacy – being desired and held in the arms of a loving man. I would allow neither cars, boats, planes nor trains to entice me and take me off my course.

What I found most demoralizing and demeaning was to be considered as a "side piece," or, God forbid, "a booty call" or "special friend" (a woman who was to be called at a whim's notice for 'whatever' sexual escapade the caller fancied). There were many who, sensing they couldn't hold that special place in my heart, proposed to me that they become my "Spiritual Mentor," "Counselor," or "Advisor." Didn't matter the title, it was still the same thing. If I had to hide under the cloak of darkness and night and couldn't speak of it to my family or friends, then a "side piece" and "booty call" was what I was. And, thanks, but no thanks. My warning was clear from my childhood and those two women in the two units of our apartment complex.

LESSONS LEARNED FROM BLOOD LINES

There were pain-filled and hurtful family issues that had nothing to do with things I, myself, had actually done, or failed to do. But they were those issues that flowed from my husband's bloodlines and mine. Issues that we fell victim to and that were being perpetuated in our lifestyles. These, too, threatened to overtake my children and me. The most troubling of these disclosures being that at the time of their impending deaths, I learned that the men in my family had established what was known by all, the disgrace of 'having had sex with every young girl in their town." And I couldn't. No, I wouldn't have it said of me that I gave the last of my life to having sex with a multitude of different men. It mattered not whether those men were single or married. Sure, I was easy pickings - living alone, without a visible love interest, and obviously still very interested in sex. But, with the memory of those ancestors' end, whoever cared to come and try to "shake that thing" as hard as they could, would not be able to budge it. Cause I wasn't biting.

Sure, even though many women were having multiple children from multiple different men, I had broken that curse in my family and my children had been freed as well. However, the price I had to pay by staying with Marshall... Our children were all grown and gone now, so I didn't have the threat or the pressure of inflicting "Baby Mama Drama" into my life to get whatever resources I needed. I was now a woman beyond the years of bearing children, barring a miracle from God, so I was eternally grateful to Him for sparing me this. What I had done years before in marrying Marshall was to be covered by God's

"Permissive Will." I now had to "know" that the CHOICE WAS GOD'S "Perfect Will" for me. It was the only way to be certain that I had "passed" my test.

PROPHESIED: "WILL BE AN EXAMPLE TO WOMEN"

It had been prophesied that I "would be an example to teach a lesson to young women and old alike." Those were the words spoken by a man who was prophesying during a ceremony where I thought we were lined up to receive words of blessing and direction for our lives. I should have known better, when Marshall's intended new wife got in line right beside me. It was the two of us left standing and she would receive the declaration over her life first. As I listened intently, hers was pretty much the same as I received. We were both to be examples and our lives would be a testament to other women and to God's glory. I pondered his added words to me, "A lesson that would teach them, all women." Those words carried the tone of me bearing retribution and judgment.

THEIR EYES WERE WATCHING HER

All eyes were watching me too. All these many years later women from every conceivable area of influence and association I was involved in or connected to wanted to see how I would live the life of a widow who had gone against society's grain and who now had men attracted to and running after her. Daughters could see the looks their dads gave me. Wives sat ever closer to their husbands whenever I was around. And the single women made sure I wasn't invited to any of their "Single's" functions; especially where single brothers would be in attendance. There were those, too, who were looking to see if I would pull another stunt like the one I had pulled with their sorority sister.

That period when I left Marshall after about six years of "I can't do this foolishness anymore" and returned to my hometown is when I took up a relationship that I had toyed with, prior to getting married and moving away. I had fought hard to not become involved, fearing it would cause me to affirm everything in myself that I thought I needed and desired at that time. It offered me temporary prestige, honor, emotional and physical fulfillment, along with increased financial resources – all under the cover of a "kept woman." I would be at his disposal - ready at a whim's notice. And I thought that so long as my physical and emotional needs were being met, such a relationship would be something I would love.

There were functions he insisted I be at, but always under the watchful eye and protection of one he had appointed as my escort. He would introduce the both of us, and it was oh so obvious that there was something else going on between the two of us – he and I. Which may be why I could detect that there was more to Marshall and my Esther's introduction. The eyes he gave me, most times, my being the youngest thing in the room were unmistakable – and embarrassing. That he chose to wink and lick his lips non-stop while gazing directly at me didn't convince anyone that there was nothing going on. So these thirty-plus years later, many of those women were still around and they were watching to see if I would pull my same old antics again. "Once a _ _,' always a _ _" was the chant I would overhear in hallways and corridors, so many times.

Thing was, there was one of their husbands who was actually interested in me and he fit every qualification of my unwritten "HE SO FINE" criteria - exactly and to the "T." Had I looked for someone to "hook up with" in prior years, he would have more than fit the bill. He and I would have more than 'tripped the light fantastic." Every part of my body wanted to "skip the light fandango" with this woman's husband, several times, and for as many times and as often as I could. Yes, Lord! He did that to me and for me, and more. He was intelligent, super book-smart, tall, handsome, and -- not afraid to talk to me or to touch me. And, a critically important thing at this time was, I was super-attracted to him too, and in the very worst way.

But, I couldn't. It was that dreaded fear of violating another woman's marriage that kept me from betraying my commitment. God had forgiven me for my foolish act with that other woman's husband years ago and allowed me to endure and triumph over my experience with My Esther. So it mattered not that I knew that man desired me as much as I did him. I gladly endured the pain of walking away from the only man who, up to that point in my life, had brought tears to my eyes at the mere thought of never being with him.

When the desire to be with him was so overwhelming that I felt I could no longer control myself, is when I had to repeat, repeat, repeat, and repeat again, with tears drenching my eyes and face my God-given mantra. Although I was sure ours was fueled by much more than our flesh or lusts, I could not allow myself to entertain the possibility that we could be the answer to both our heart's desires. I couldn't allow myself to entertain that surely we could ask God for his covering and he would answer us. But, what of his wife? So, though the cost to me was so painful, I ran away repeating, "I will not forfeit the Divine Purpose and Plan God has for my life for the temporal, soulish, flesh-driven, and lust-filled desires, pleasures, fornications and whoredoms of this world" for as many times as necessary until... my longing and desire, felt in every fiber of my body, for that one, had passed. It didn't help knowing that he felt the same way about me. If he only knew that the one and only thing keeping us apart was a commitment and promise I had made with the Father, then he too would honor and respect it. Or... would he rationalize our attraction and come up with some type concession that gave us the liberty to explore our cravings? If that were the case, I could never let him know my true feelings. So, aside from the obvious, but uncontrollable doe-eyed stares I gave him whenever our eyes met, he would never know. It was now that I would have to keep it together, girl!

(Wipe away the tears!)
Repeat the Mantra!
(Dry those eyes!)
Repeat!!!
(Remember the Assignment!)
And Repeat again!
(God's got you!)
Guard and Focus, Girl!

His Word and His Promises are True and Sure!

So, to all those on-lookers, the young women, wives, widows (and the men associated with them), I had to show them all, that I was never a threat. Though it meant denying myself of a relationship that promised to be fulfilling and satisfying in every way I had ever hoped for or desired.

That great crowd would all wonder why it was I seemed to be "missing it," "missing out" and not "taking advantage of" all the "opportunities" being presented before me. Why it was I had not chosen any of the ones who had come for me. The ones who, upon learning I was more "in need" than had "resources to offer as a dowry of sorts"; had made me to feel they would just as soon have me licking their boots than sharing their hearts emotions and desires with me.

A "PASS AROUND GIRL"

Then, there were those who offered to have me become their "prize" to be used to appease all their sexual needs and desires. My payment would be having my financial needs taken care of, sure. These ones could very well see how much I still desired physical contact as well. So, in payment, they would all take their "turn" with me. They had no idea that God had done a real work in me to have me process all that had transpired in my mind and heart regarding what it was those sisters in the units of our apartment strip were up to. If it had not been for God having me to see and understand, I would most likely have eagerly and willingly entertained their proposal - becoming most accommodating and compliant. BUT GOD!

Upon witnessing the hurt and pain of my own children in observing the shenanigans of their father as he entertained acquiring another and "new" wife, I could in no way consider or be complicit in what these fathers and husbands, were contemplating. They all had young ones who would experience the very same hurts and disappointments my own children had -- and all for the sake of fulfilling their sexual fantasies and desires with me. No amount of anticipated fulfillment of those desires or needs could bring me to cause such devastating feelings and emotions in the hearts of other children. Nothing was worth that. So, No. I would not be a pass-around chick for any amount of money.

Then, it was not for money; it was not for the companionship of another woman's husband; nor was it for the fulfillment of physical needs and desires that could cause me to abandon the path I had been given by my Father. I did realize that by my taking these positions, I had officially caused myself to tie my own hands behind my back. There appeared to be no way that a relationship of any type could qualify by the criteria that had been set. By accepting God's path to fulfill the assignment on my life, I was employing the very restrictions that prevented me from crossing the lines that He Himself had drawn. It was settled, then. I was not going to go against what my God had allowed me to see were the places I had failed him before. I was not going to be bound by the actions of embittered and painful circumstances of my youth, or by past failed relationships, or by the material enticements of this world. I was now a woman way past the age of being considered desirable, or of having the fame, notoriety or wealth that bought attention. So, there appeared no way possible that I could, or would, be considered worthy of ever being "found" by a redeemer. BUT GOD!

CHAPTER FIVE

GRACE RESTORATION

When the king asked the woman, she related it to him.
So the king appointed for her a certain officer, saying,
"RESTORE ALL that was hers and all the produce of the field from
the day that she left the land even until NOW."
2Kings 8:6

If you are pure and upright, Surely now He would rouse Himself
for you and RESTORE your righteous estate. "Though your
BEGINNING was insignificant, Yet your END will increase
greatly.
Job 8:6-7

God the Father knew you and chose you long ago, and his Spirit
has made you holy. As a result, you have obeyed him and have
been cleansed by the blood of Jesus Christ. May God give you
more and more GRACE and peace.
1Peter 1:2

May God our Father and the Lord Jesus Christ
give you GRACE and peace...GRACE to you and peace from
God our Father and the Lord Jesus Christ.
2Thes 1:2, 2Cor 1:2, Eph. 1:2, Phil. 1:2, Col 1:2

For it is by GRACE you have been saved, through FAITH—and
this is not from yourselves, it is the GIFT OF GOD.
Ephesians 2:8

REVELATION

Then, it came to me just as I had completed that final purging and deliverance from my life's failures and family curses. I resolved that no redemption was ever possible for me or choice of a mate based on any criteria I conceived of. I could in no way make a choice based on any qualities of those who showed interest in me. It became perfectly clear to me that I was exactly right. Based on all those carnal factors I was looking at, judgment said, "There is no way."

So, I finally conceded and realized that the choice of a new mate, my Redeemer, wasn't my decision to make at all. Freedom! I recognized I would have never been able to receive the gift that "the one who her heart desired" was, unless I had explicitly followed God's plan. To be finally and fully cleansed and purified of all guilt, shame, hurt, and pain, willful and wanton acts of defiance, disobedience, ignorance and arrogance. That was the gift he had for me, His Grace. No, I didn't deserve any of what I desired when judged based on my actions. But God's grace was without my having to do a thing except, accept it! His plan all along was that I would be humbled and by prayer, would seek his face, would turn from my wicked ways and it would be then that he would hear me and forgive me, and restore to me. (2Chron 7:14) This was the plan, the map for me and everyone desiring to be made right in him.

Once acknowledging my faults, sinfulness, and shortcomings, my slate had to be totally cleansed and cleared. I would have never been able to do it on my own. It was realizing that nothing I could have done or said to anyone at any time could have done the work in my life that was needed. Realizing that the price for my getting to the place I was now had been paid long, long ago. It was a gift that was mine for the taking. I only had to accept it. There was absolutely nothing I could do to earn it and it could not be bought.

This Vashti finally realized she couldn't perform any act good enough or behave well enough to merit it. It was free for the taking by a heart that was submitted, surrendered, cleansed, and purified by the Word of God. It was hers by God's Unmerited, Undeserved, Unearned grace and favor. She had endured and suffered through her life's adversities so that what emerged was a heart and soul cleansed from every guilty stain of sin by the blood of the Sacrificial Lamb.

I had made it! I had survived my trials and tests. I had a few shaky moments there, for sure. In addition, I was a little worn and tattered - even had a limp in my walk (Gen. 32:24-32) having wrestled and battled - but triumphed. God had shown me the path (Psalm 16:11) I had to take and now it was time for me to rest and receive all His promises.

I had also found the key to the question, "How was I to choose a mate?" Knowing it had nothing whatsoever to do with me making a choice but it was more a "good" thing when a man "finds a wife" and obtains favor of the Lord. (Prov. 18:22). The operative words being "good," "man finds," and "wife." Whew! That took all the work off my shoulders! My Kinsman Redeemer was going to find me. And all I had to do and be was prepared and ready to receive Him. Yes, it did create a dilemma for me that I had absolutely nothing to offer - no money, no house, no career with income potential; nothing. But when I considered another heroine of the Old Testament, Ruth, I took careful notes of what that woman had to offer that caused Boaz to take notice of her.

Ruth was devoted and committed to her mother-in-law Naomi, and to Naomi's God. She refused to turn back to her old ways, her family or her country. She was consistent in the work she was able to perform and did it willingly and did not bemoan her circumstances as a gleaner. Ruth had a heart, respect and compassion for the old and infirm, her mother-in-law. And finally, Ruth followed the advice and directives of her mentor, mother-in-law. Never could I have gotten to this place without going through all the years of preparation of learning to love when everything in me said to feel otherwise. How would I ever know how to receive true love if I had not witnessed first-hand deception and lies? How would I know the true touch and look of love and desire if I hadn't first honored my body as a *"temple of the Holy Spirit" residing in me, which was "given as a gift by God..." and not abused it as my own.* (1Cor 6:19 KJV, NIV, NASB, AMP)

In addition, how could a loving God ever have honored me by making me one who "was pleasing" and one in which "favor was found." It could have never happened if I had dishonored and chosen to violate the relationships of all the women whose husbands, boyfriends, and fiancés' had set their sights on me.

REVEALING

I had only my dress left to put on before he came to collect me. There were no problems or trials to what I was faced with today. This was a time, a day of true rejoicing. Finally, this would be the Complete Restoration of my Relationships, Finances and matters of my heart - my Romance. And it was all to be done at one time. The fruit of my hands would reverse my past days of unfruitfulness, non-productivity, and would begin my career and calling. All was to be established and restored because of my faithfulness, obedience, and perseverance. Sure, all the "things" I was now set to receive were great; but, the best thing of all was HIM. My greatest heart's desire fulfilled.

Throughout all the heartache and pain the humiliation and shame, the abandonment, rejection, and loneliness - I had made it, and I was now at this place of God's Promise. What it had taken to get here was a whole "'notha ordeal." Those massive life dilemmas created whirlwinds of problems that hadn't been any fun at all – but were oh so necessary. Their unveiling, and then my eventually facing and dealing with them head-on is what God desired for their total resolution.

It was now that I would finally get to see – Him. No, I had not yet seen his face – not in person that is. My spirit had long ago shown me who he was, but I just couldn't go before God granted me permission. I would wait for the Lord to reveal him.

Even our wedding ceremony had been a masterful depiction of two souls committed to God's Will, Purpose and

Plan. I had been led down the aisle to a breathtaking altar arch. I would have to find out later which flowers they used for the colors purple and bronze, they were amazingly gorgeous. Those colors that signified we had been judged as ones "close to God's heart," purple; and as ones who were "judged righteous," the bronze.

I felt myself slowing down to take in the beauty of what I was seeing, but was gently nudged to keep moving forward, to my journey's end. This wedding altar had been separated down the center with my husband-to-be standing on the opposite side of the veil that served as the separation. He would be able to hear my voice recite the vows that were uniting us into a life of mutual love and devotion. His voice would be that of someone else. My commitment to this marriage was to be made totally dependent upon God's choosing - and I was perfectly alright, just fine, with that. All kisses and exchange of rings would be done later when he came to the place he was to get to know me.

And now that time had finally come. What I had seen many times before was a vision of a broad-faced smile that radiated light. I had been drawn to the light of that huge smile with the knowing in my spirit that it belonged to someone who would be associated with "marriage and union" - and I would be involved. That vision had come at a time when all hell was breaking loose in my marriage to Marshall so I felt initially that it was the assurance from God that there was another who would share in life with me love, laughter, and joy - finally. But back then, I had not yet learned to fully understand how God revealed His messages to me. So, I just placed that dream into my mental basket and filed it along with so many of the others. My trust was in the hope that one day the fullness of the meaning of who that man with that smile was would eventually be revealed. That day was now – today - because "He" was actually about to come through that door.

To think that he was the one who had seen the woman I had been, and waited for me to become the woman I now was - healed, delivered, made whole, purpose-filled and restored, nothing missing, nothing lacking and nothing broken. He had been with me – well, actually not physically with me -- but there, in the background all along interceding and keeping me lifted up in prayer, reminding me to be encouraged throughout the process I had to go through. He was there on the sidelines, cheering me on so that I couldn't attribute any of what God was doing in my life, to what he – a mere man – would have or could have done. He had to know that my greatest desire was to know God and to know that I had an unshakable and immovable relationship with Him, the Almighty God.

He confessed to me that his mind had been made up the first time he had set eyes on me. However, he never let on his intentions throughout all our interactions. He was the one who had seen me in the stench and filth of my trying life situations and circumstances. He had witnessed me struggle to untangle and free myself from the generational curses, snares, challenges, and obstacles. He had evidenced my transformation, and stood silently by me as I was freed from the baggage, strongholds, hindrances, fears, uncertainties, and insecurities.

He was even there as the generational curses and ungodly soul ties were broken that had tried desperately to cling and hold onto me, all in an effort to prevent me from completing the transforming and renewing of my mind. All those things, the hindrances and wicked spiritual forces assigned as enemies to my destiny that were working so hard to impede my full and final deliverance that I would be kept back from the blessings that were waiting for me. I had to recognize those situations as a battle for my very faith. It was that faith in God that would be critically needed to allow me to endure to the end.

He was there throughout it all and he was the one who had won my heart over all the others. He saw me in my former unrefined state and knew that beneath that rough, calloused, and stone-hard exterior was a heart nearly at the place of cracking, breaking, and forever shattering into a million pieces. Behind its super-fortified guard-wall, was a heart of flesh longing to be loved in the only way that a true Man of God could. He saw a heart that was moldable and pliable. He was the one to make it his job to get to know the "me" behind all my protective and defensive layers I had hidden behind and more importantly, those God had wrapped me up and hidden me in -- wrapped up and hidden in, Himself. What it took for me to realize that he was that one, who "found his good thing" in me, was that journey that I would not subscribe or suggest to anyone else – friend or foe. It was on a path that would usher in the promises God had made to me.

So, I was to spend my time in this room - our wedding suite - preparing for, Him. A smile always broke out on my face whenever I thought of Him. He thought the world of my smile too. It made a special connection for us. There was a grin that would overtake my face whenever I found myself in his presence. It was that kind of grin that dating services say you should give to a man to let him know you are interested. Well, I didn't want to come off as flirty or forward, but the muscles of my face just did their own thing whenever I was around him.

So, here I sat in this beautiful room and waited for the one who had set all this up, my Beloved, *"The One whom My Soul Loved."* (Song of Solomon 1:7) It was he who had paid the ultimate price for my redemption and saved me from spending the rest of my life alone, never to experience the simple joy of male companionship or love - to say nothing of intimacy - ever again. It was he who saw me as his "good thing" – someone more than good enough and worthy of being called his "wife." (Proverbs 18:22)

No, we had never before experienced the benefit of extended periods of one-on-one personal time together where we communicated face-to-face on issues of an intimate and private nature. Ours were the written and unspoken words we transmitted to each other that allowed us still to know one another's heart. A communication process built solely on and through his writings to me and mine to him - still, love-filled initiations and responses. That method told me even more than any face-to-face interactions could have ever revealed. His love and respect for me was in every letter, every word, and every phrase. Such assurance of renewed hope and faith that, as God was the strength of our salvation, His greatest delight was in leading us both onto paths traversed by the righteous that we would both walk in the ways of the good. (Proverbs 2:20) Yes, even God himself was delighting in our upcoming union.

He was beyond anything I had ever thought I could allow myself to dream of, or hope for, in a man. And he was… all man. He, too, had undergone a number of life-changing, soul-searching, and character-building trials and challenges that would see him transformed into the man God needed him to be. His asking me to be his wife would mean he would be saying, "I will" in the ceremony instead of "I do." He would have to have an understanding of me that transcended traditional marriage roles. His would have to be one where he would need a tolerance and patience that would go far beyond the normal marriage where two partners were being united who each brought something, hopefully of equal value and worth, into the marriage union. What I had to bring was little to nothing. Nothing except the potential for greatness from what had been held up on the inside of me. There were stories, songs, poems, and business and ministry ideas – all untapped.

He was to either accept the fact that I was bringing nothing – thereby accepting me -- or, he could reject the whole notion and idea. What he saw in me was a value and worth that far outweighed any monetary or financial wealth I did or did not possess. There was a prophetic covenant he was fulfilling and I was the only one who fit the bill. He knew that. I knew that. And most importantly, God knew that. So whether I had anything to be brought to the table at this time or not, mattered none the least to him and made him "no never mind."

His most obvious and endearing qualities, to me, were that he was considerate, thoughtful, understanding, attentive, loyal, giving, observant, and communicative. Whew! All that in one "f–i– i–i–ne" package of a man! Most revealing was that he, too, gave such care to observe and pay closer than close, detailed attention to, me. But the way he did it was so much more comprehensive and detailed. He studied me so intimately and with the intention that he too, *"would learn to live with her in an understanding way."* (1 Peter 3:7). That "her," was "me." Hot dog! And all Glory to God! I could shout all day on that one.

My husband-to-be had studied what that scripture entailed so very carefully and intricately and I, me, my little ole self, was the beneficiary of all he had gleaned. Moreover, unlike my late husband Marshall, my heavenly gift of this Mighty Man of God was a true "man's man." He not only knew how to "handle his business" interacting with professionals on all business-related matters, but he had no problem whatsoever being in charge, commanding and taking complete control and being the lead.

He had 'popped the question,' proposing in one of his many messages to me. The words he chose were written articulately, skillfully, and most carefully – IN ALL CAPS. HE WAS SERIOUS! As I read those words, my heart leaped, pounding louder at each letter, word, and phrase of MARRY ME. Such a well-thought out expression and display of his amazing love and affection for me blew me away.

YOU ARE WHO I HAVE BEEN PRAYING TO GOD FOR

MARRY ME!

I HAVE WANTED YOU SINCE THE VERY FIRST
TIME I SAW YOU.
I CAN'T THINK CLEARLY WHEN I'M
AWAY FROM YOU AND EVEN LESS FOCUSED
WHEN WE ARE TOGETHER
(BUT MY HEART IS SO MUCH HAPPIER)
MARRY ME!
YOUR SMILE MAKES EVERYTHING
ALL RIGHT FOR ME,
YOUR GRIN,
(SINFUL AND DEVIOUS AS IT IS)
I NOTICE YOU NEVER, EVER USE IT
WITH ANYONE ELSE,
IT IS ONLY FOR ME.
MARRY ME!
I WON'T BE PERFECT, BUT I'LL BE ALL YOURS.
MARRY ME!
THERE IS NOTHING ABOUT YOU THAT I AM NOT
GRATEFUL TO GOD FOR!
AS I HAVE WATCHED YOU
WALK EVERY STEP OF YOUR PATH TO
WHOLENESS AND COMPLETENESS, YOU HAVE
SHOWN THAT YOUR HEART IS FULLY DEVOTED
AND DEDICATED TO OUR GOD.
I LOVE YOU FOR THAT.
MARRY ME!
NOW!

I could hear his voice speaking those words and all of me lit up. I didn't know it was possible to feel a smile all on the inside of myself, but every fiber of my being was infused with "happy." I could see him getting so excited and carried away as he wrote out each word, losing himself in the moment. I was sure, as he was sure, that our being together was what we both were destined for - desperately needed and wanted. Ours was a controlled, yet raw and primal hunger and desire for each other that had stood the test of time and was now to be fulfilled - without inhibition or reserve.

As our reward for patiently waiting for our "God Reveal" and learning as much as possible about each other through the seemingly restrictive means of social media, we had developed a respect for one another's virtue and commitment to celibacy. We still managed to share many episodes of passion-filled encounters, albeit by laptop and tablet keyboard. He had never behaved like anything less than a gentleman's gentleman and, sight unseen, I had never doubted that he would be an engaging and satisfying lover.

BRIDAL SUITE

It was in this dream bridal suite that I waited for the door to open revealing the one who had paid it all for me – my "Redeemer." It was he I had allowed the walls of my heart to be broken down for (Ezekiel 11:19) and who I had placed all my faith and trust in to "cherish and love me like Christ loved His Church."(Ephesians 5:29) It was he, who was the only one worthy of my having waited and prepared myself for. In this magnificent hotel suite, I would finally get to see – Him.

So, now, here I sat, fixated by, obsessed with, and absorbed in feelings of a mixture of amazement and stupefied wonder and awe. This palatial Presidential Penthouse Suite pristinely bedecked and decorated throughout with varying hues of the two colors that had become what was past being an obsession for me. Whenever I thought of them, it was as if they were running through my veins, filling and infusing every ounce of my being. With my every breath, I felt it transverse throughout my entire body. The only thing in my memory to be even remotely as breathtaking, was the scene in The Color Purple when, during Celie and her sister Nettie's reunion, they were enveloped in a sea of purple blossoms. Purple, "the color closest to God's heart." That is where I felt I was at this time, too - close to the heart of God. The fullness of this beautifully decorated and accented room all gave affirmation to this being a place of dignity and honor – as I had been promised.

The Bronze Metallic had been problematic for me when I first researched that it symbolized "judgment." But, God had affirmed that I had indeed been through a time of judgment. And for coming through triumphantly, the promise made to restore me for surviving those seasons of unimaginable pain, embarrassment, and shame was now to be fulfilled.

There were purple and bronze metallic flower-filled vases, coordinating crisp bed linens, and window drapes with the whitest of white sprinkles of furnishings and room accessories throughout. This room far exceeded the one in my vision as I looked out the wall-to-wall glass-encased windows overlooking the pallid sands and baby blue waters. This secluded, private-owned Caribbean island beachfront seemed made just for me. None of what I was now experiencing could my once small mind ever even conceive of. But, getting a vision of the BIG God had for me, see it most clearly now. Yet, in the most tender nudging in my spirit, I could hear God say, *"You knew I was 'able' to do EXCEEDING ABUNDANTLY ABOVE all that you asked or could even think of... "* (Ephesians 3:20)

I had "made it." Now was my time to prepare myself for "HIM." After a long and luxurious bath and the pampering by the hotel's Massage attendants, my hair had been done just as He had conveyed to me He envisioned it. It was now time to apply my makeup. He had insisted I have it done professionally -- something I had never experienced before. I rather considered myself a makeup aficionado and cherished the opportunities I had to experiment on myself. But, for today, I was "directed" to place myself in the hands of those sent to "prepare" me for Him. He was bossy like that - not controlling or overbearing – and I loved it. He "took charge" of the major affairs of our lives (and some little ones like insisting I allow myself to be pampered) – and boy, oh boy did I love him even more for it.

It was no difficulty at all giving over the decision to God of who would be selected as the one I would give my heart to. Because the Father had brought me through such a testing of my faith, I trusted Him completely. He knew best who it was that accepted the "tore up from the floor up" mess that I had been. God's judgment I trusted for the One who would love and cherish me, for me - just like He, God, Himself had.

So as I caught the sound of the footsteps coming up the hallway, my heart seemed to explode in anticipation of just who it would be to enter that door. Yes, even though we had only communicated by Email and Face Book, InstaGram and Twitter - never did we have a face-to-face interaction where I knew that he was "the one." And that was fine with me. I was fully resolved and content to await my big day of reveal. Although I was sure, I had a pretty good idea who it would be and felt positive I had been personally close to him, possibly many times. Still yet, I didn't know for sure if he was the one communicating with me. And I would never betray the trust of the Father by attempting to uncover who His choice would be for me.

Even so, I felt I would know him as if we were life-long friends. I had no apprehension whatsoever, because no one had ever, or could ever love me like my God had and he had promised to give me a love for all time. No, I had never seen him to know that he was God's Best Choice for me, but I could sense His presence always abiding with me. He was like my God in that I knew he was always somewhere around watching after my every concern and need. He never left me nor forsook me.

The door's handle was being turned and as my husband-to-be stepped into our room, a smile came to my face that showed my utter satisfaction and pleasure with who He was - the deepest desire of my heart, fulfilled. We would spend most of the night talking and feeling one another out.

It was he who first crossed that boundary that in times past had been set by God. It felt so right now that it was okay to cross it. He touched my hand, ever so innocently. It seemed to startle both him and me. An electric shock coursed through both our bodies. I didn't know how we would ever make it to our marriage bed. We would most likely totally ignite one another afire just from the energy of our built-up passions. I didn't know about him, but I was about to pass completely out. This all was way too much for me to handle.

He was such a solid specimen of a man. I had touched his arm as we laughed about some joke of his, and must have looked some kind of silly. In response, my eyes bulged and my body exploded in an unexpected release of a flood of pure sensual ecstasy and delight. It felt amazing! My thighs in typical reflex, squeezed together hoping to savor the feeling, but I tried to collect myself and recover hoping this man couldn't see that it took so little to arouse that side of this woman. I don't think I pulled it off, but he was a gentleman and grinned softly at me while raising one brow. He was priming himself for the take down. My body was saying there would be many of those, so Lord help us both.

As the sun came into the room, I was in his arms with my head lying across his shoulder. I realized we had talked until the next morning, we were still in our clothes from the night before. It was real and not a dream. I must have watched him as he slept there for what felt to me like an hour or more shaking my head and blinking my eyes in disbelief. Watching his chest rise and fall with each of his heartbeats. I let my heart's rhythm sync with his and that must have been what awakened him – the power and force from our two hearts beating as one. It began with the corners of his mouth spreading and then there it was, that toothy smile I had seen before. His first words to me were, "Good Morning, The ONLY ONE who pleases me and who I find great favor with." Our eyes met and locked. I could "see him" through his eyes. All my being melted in relief. He was The One. "THANK YOU GOD!"

GOD'S DIVINE PURPOSE AND PLAN
& PROPHECIES... FULFILLED

Still, if it had not been for the life challenges I had to face, I would not have made it to this place; in the arms of "The One My Heart Desired, My Beloved." This was the part of my dreams I was most happy to retain and recall over and over again. The beauty of all I was enveloped in totally engrossed me. It was at this place where the light appeared at the end of that dark road and all the tears dried up. This is when I again heard the voice, "You have reached the place I intended for you. All that you desire is now yours - complete restoration of all. But none of those things compare to the greatest gift I have for you. You have fought well to change the characteristics describing your name, Iva. I declare to you that no longer will you be identified as one "overturned, ruined, or conquered;" nor considered as the symbol for a pagan god."

"Moses declared to you who I was, the "I Am." To Isaiah I gave to declare that the nations would see my righteousness and all the kings my glory and you should be called by a "new name" that I, the Lord, would give you. (Isa. 62:2, 4) But John the Revelator recorded in my book that I would declare to the one who was victorious, that I would make him a pillar in my temple and give to him a white stone. I would write on that stone "my own new name" and the name of my city. Also, my child, not only on that white stone, but II would write on that one who is victorious "my own new name."

(Rev. 3:12) You have earned your white stone that bears the engraving of my own new name that until I released you to write and reveal that vision, only you knew and only understood, IVAH."

It was my hearing that name as he spoke it that caused me to take in a deep breath and as I released it, I felt a disconnection of that bond I had developed with Queen Vashti. Yes, I had been wrapped up in the drama, complicity and turmoil of her life's choices, but no longer. I had DIVINELY COMPLETED AND FULFILLED the Assignment on my life and had n*ot Forfeited that Purpose and Plan God had for me in exchange for any Temporal, Soul-ish, Flesh-Driven, or Lust-Filled Desires, Pleasures, Fornications or Whoredoms of this World!* I was released and restored.

He was right, that still small voice. I did understand. On Christ, the solid rock I'd stood freed from my past, the white of the stone signifying my cleansing and purging. I did understand my new name and his new name, and it was powerful.

I had been especially chosen for situations and experiences many would not have tolerated ending up with such a deep and abiding love for the Father and a determination to stick with it, and never give in or give up. It was his assurances by confirmations of dreams and visions and faith and trust in his Word that had caused all things indeed to work together for good.

And then, to finally get to a place where I, by my lifestyle and my conduct was an example to unmarried - young and old; divorced and widowed, women. It was how Father God would have us to walk through our times of singlehood, widowhood, years after divorce and years between marriages. My life became a living epistle and could very well have been titled, "The Woman of the Last Book." As a widow, I had been sent as a witness to the people of God to attest to whether the work The Father had sent his son to them for would be exhibited in how they received and dealt with her. I believe the Father would be greatly pleased to know that His people got it. They understood that His Grace and Mercy covers all.

@IVAHFRISONASHE   @IVAFRISONASHE

@FRISONASHE   @REDEEMINGVASHTI   @IVAH

REDEEMINGVASHTI@GMAIL.COM

www.redeemingvashti.com

www.ivahfrisonashe.com